Challenge

En Souvenir,

Frédéric Giovel

1980

By Frédéric Lionel

ROMANS INITIATIQUES
Editions La Baconnière
L'Etreinte des Masques.
L'Affrontement.
Au Diapason Secret.
L'Emprise de l'Etrange.

OUVRAGES PHILOSOPHIQUES
Editions Robert Laffont
Présence de la Grande Tradition.
L'Accessible du Merveilleux.
L'Enigme que nous sommes.
Le Tarot Initiatique (en préparation).

ESSAIS PHILOSOPHIQUES
Editions de Bassaraba
La Philosophie des Nombres, l'Hermétisme et les Problèmes de notre Temps.
L'Astrologie Sacrée, Voie de l'Initiation aux Choses de la Vie.
La Voie du Dépassement.
Réflexions sur des Sujets Essentiels.
L'Attrait de l'Occulte.
La Quête de l'Intemporel.

OUVRAGE en LANGUE ALLEMANDE
Editeur: Reichl Verlag-Remagen
Abendland Hüter der Flamme.

Challenge

by

FREDERIC LIONEL

On Special Mission

with a Foreword by
Sir George Trevelyan Bt. M.A.

SUFFOLK
NEVILLE SPEARMAN

First Published in Great Britain in 1980 by
Neville Spearman Limited
The Priory Gate, Friars Street, Sudbury, Suffolk

©Frédéric Lionel

First published in France in 1976
under the title
Un Chemin sur la Braise
© 1976 Charles-Lavauzelle, Limoges

ISBN 85435 354 2

Printed and bound in Great Britain by
Biddles Ltd, Guildford and King's Lynn

Foreword

BY SIR GEORGE TREVELYAN Bt. M.A.

This book offers an admirable tale of war-time adventure. It is the personal story of one who went with great courage through four years of the Underground Movement in France and came through it unscathed. Frédéric Lionel, a Frenchman speaking German perfectly, offered his services to the British Government to start a rescue service for escape to England from occupied France. Thus he was one of the very first to initiate and develop the link with the Fifth Column and the Undergound Movement in France. Trained as a Commando in Scotland, he became a Major of the British Army. He has now written the story of his adventures, which will throw a vivid light on the period from 1940-44. It reads somewhat like the deeds of the Scarlet Pimpernel.

But in addition to being a gripping tale of true adventure, this book has a deeper significance which will appeal to all concerned with esoteric knowledge and the movement for quickening of the spirit in our time. For Frédéric Lionel is a sensitive and adept, with deep knowledge of the Ageless Mystery-Wisdom. This he teaches through seminars and conferences in Europe and now in England at a series of Wrekin Trust events.

He sees his war-time experience in France as a training. He became clearly aware that he was being led and taught by invisible guides working through his own Higher Self. This involved his developing a highly sensitized intuition which would enable him to respond instantly with total obedience to the promptings of the 'still small voice' within his own mind and heart. He says that he had to make himself 'Tout a fait disponable' — absolutely available and subservient to the inner guide and teacher.

He saw that in order to be able to react instantly under the guidance of his Higher Self into totally new and unexpected

i

circumstances, he had to jettison old beliefs and habit patterns and learn to obey his intuition implicitly in split-second reactions. This capacity is well illustrated in the adventures here described.

It is a power which in some degree we shall all need to develop. Those concerned with the spiritual awakening in our time are increasingly aware that the primary task is to find the inner teacher and submit to this guidance in free creative activity. Indeed here lies the clue which is going to prove vitally important if we are to move courageously and creatively through the times of great change which we are approaching. We must expect inner changes of consciousness and with it in all probability outer changes in society and even world structure. We must see this as part of the cleansing of our polluted planet, as a necessary prelude to the birth of a new age. 'Behold, I make all things new'. If we can grasp this tremendous picture we shall move forward into the future with high-hearted courage and hope. But it will mean our all learning to live creatively in the moment under the certainty that we are in truth being led by an invisible guidance working through the very centre of our consciousness. Then life will increasingly become an adventure into the unknown and the new, knowing that we are always shown one step ahead and are being led into situations staged by the invisible world for our training and for the building of soul-strength. So life becomes an adventure in co-operation with the powers of Light, which may be called the angelic forces of the Archangel Michael and of the Christ, the Lord of Light. With Paul we must learn to say 'I live, yet not I, but Christ lives in me'.

It is as if all who are concerned with the spiritual understanding are members of a Fifth Column working in an enemy occupied country. We have picked up the signals of impending invasion. 'Operation Redemption' has been launched and the Forces of Light are coming. Each individual and group can be a point in our darkened planet sending up a signal light to guide the incoming parachutists. The analogy of war is often powerful in describing the spiritual situation. It seems certain that we are being trained for great events in the transformation of mankind in the next twenty years. There never was such a generation in which to be alive.

Thus Frédéric Lionel's war-time experience can be read as an illustration of how the higher worlds can train a man. He had to go through his adventures in order to make a break-through in consciousness and learn co-operation with the Masters of Wisdom. His book may be read simply as an enthralling tale of war-time experience and an interesting picture of how the Resistance Movement developed, but it can also help all on the spiritual path to understand and practise the nature of training in creative obedience to our invisible guides.

I warmly recommend the book to all concerned with the 'consciousness movement'. It is the personal story of a brave man serving the cause of light through times of peril.

PREFACE

I wrote this book not merely to describe shattering events which almost destroyed a world I believed to be safe. I wrote it to make people aware that the most dramatic experiences may lead to a vision of the problems of life, thereby unveiling a path to happiness. For obvious reasons, certain names of persons and places have been changed.

1

'Don't turn back if you want to discover life. The past is gone, and the path leads forward.' These were my father's last words to me before leaving me forever. I understand his wisdom. Yet I must now turn back so as to remember how certain events happened and how deeply they influenced not only my destiny but my vision of the world.

I want to begin this story with the words 'Once upon a time...' Although it is not a fairy-tale, yet I can imagine that, at my birth, kind fairies bestowed blessings on the new-born child.

'You will be healthy and given awareness; you will come to know the world and without having wealth you will never go hungry.'

But one fairy had been forgotten, and appearing, she thundered: 'Anything you will undertake will meet with difficulties. No easy path shall lie before you.' Having spoken these words, she left in a whirl.

Today I ask myself whether the difficulties encountered have not been the most precious gift of all. They were considerable, but none has turned out to have been in vain, and all helped foster an understanding which has led to an ever broadening consciousness. Plato says: 'The world of our vision is our prison'. It is the difficulties men have to overcome which reveal the importance of taking existence as a springboard towards understanding. My story does not provide an answer to the innumerable problems confronting each of us, I only wish to show that daily ordeals can become stepping stones into a world which has to be explored.

It is a vast world with many facets. I know how difficult it is to accept facts which exceed the limits of a rational approach, and fail to fit into the conventional setting which we have learned to enjoy. I know how painful it is to overcome one's established opinions, yet it must be done by those who would dare escape from limitation to liberty.

To be free in the true sense of the word requires courage. It is worth while and I think I can prove it. In fact, that is the object of my story.

One beautiful afternoon of September 1938, sitting on the terrace of the Cafe de la Paix on the Grands Boulevards in Paris, I bought a newspaper announcing in large headlines that the Munich agreement had been signed between Hitler, Mussolini, Chamberlain and Daladier.

A rapidly approaching brouhaha made me look up. A motorcade passed by. Daladier, standing up in an open car, visibly moved to see the Parisians rushing up to shout approval, waved and bowed to the plaudits of the crowd.

I felt deeply shaken. The illusion that war had been avoided was big enough to create a false feeling of relief which would hamper the effort indispensable to prevent the looming disaster.

I was well placed to foresee the diabolic sequence of events after the Munich capitulation, and I knew that this capitulation would be regarded by Hitler as proof of the weakness of a decadent people, ripe for domination.

I foresaw the implications clearly as I was married to a German. More than once during my long discussions with young Berliners, friends of my wife, I had felt an implacable logic, sustained by the will for domination, generated and

2

strengthened by an inferiority complex born after the defeat of 1918; a defeat which, they felt, was not deserved. Through blood and fire they were determined to glorify the German fatherland so that nobody would ever jeer again.

I had met my wife, Heidi, one summer day in the Swiss Engadine. I was sitting on the edge of the hotel swimming pool. The sun shone, the firs of the surrounding forests filled the air with their scent and I watched the movements of a ravishing creature swimming in the blue water. She had just dived from the high board and I was admiring her perfect features and form.

A little later, I approached her with a beating heart, unaware that at that moment the trajectory of my fate was about to take me off the beaten track. She was indeed beautiful, so I thought, slender and athletic but not aggressively so. An enigmatic smile gave her nordic madonna-like face, framed in hair as blond as corn that indescribable air of ingenuousness which will always disarm a man. Particularly if he has fallen in love.

Love at first sight! It happened. Heidi responded to my advances. I was twenty-five, she was twenty. I was quite good looking and had, so I told her, a brilliant future in mind. I was working at the time in a completely new field — cybernetics. This recently born science of electronics, aiming at the conquest of space, opened up incredible possibilities. At that first encounter, while talking with her of the future, I was already seeing Heidi as my wife.

A fortnight after our first meeting, I asked her to marry me. She accepted after some hesitation, and it is necessary to say that I did all I could to convince her.

The wedding took place in Berlin in 1933. In the streets, crowds were demonstrating. A 'spontaneous' demonstration organised by the leaders of the triumphant National Socialist Party had spread over the residential districts of the town. Yelling mobs were smashing the windows of shops owned by Jews or by opponents to the new regime. Passers-by, taking advantage of such a boon, were looting indiscriminately, enjoying the pillage or looking on as if taking part in a show.

They cheered the brown-shirted youths who were egging on the crowds, and acclaimed the police cars which turned a blind eye and drove on.

As we drove from the Registry Office to the Protestant church near the Kurfürstendamm, the spectacle was appalling.

Obviously, the violence was organised. Nothing seemed left to chance, the streamers, banners and flags formed the background of a stage on which a drama was performed. Nothing was spontaneous, except the tears of the insulted and terrorized victims who were forced to bear cardboard placards with vile inscriptions pinned on their clothes.

Heidi's father displaying the Iron Cross, first class, from World War I, was trying to play down the incidents which, he asserted, were acts of an ignorant minority. Heidi's mother, painfully embarrassed, hurried us home.

What appalled me was the glee on every face. How could so many men and women, belonging to such a highly civilized country, indulge in such merciless vandalism.

Heidi, a slight smile on her lips, seemed absent-minded and said little about anything. The day after the wedding, with its horribly disturbing background, we left Berlin. Returning to France, we settled at Neuilly, a suburb of Paris. Our circle of friends grew fast.

Heidi threw herself into social gaieties — not difficult in the hedonistic climate of the thirties. She was attractive and vivacious; she loved to be popular and admired. It was a whirl of madcap motoring weekends at Deauville, night clubs, dashes to the Côte d'Azur, parties here, there and everywhere.

At one of these parties we met Count Guy and his young wife, Sylvie. Twice Heidi's age, he quickly gained a complete ascendancy over her, and became her evil genius. He understood, maybe better than I did at the time, that she was torn between the urge to satisfy her unquenchable thirst for pleasure and her desire to comply with the ascetic virtues praised in the German newspapers she continued to read. With this understanding, Count Guy was able to manipulate her as he chose.

4

Two daughters were born to us during the first five years of our married life. By September 1939 the youngest was seven months old and the eldest just over four years.

Although she would not admit it, the Hitlerian ideal of glory as promised to German youth strongly attracted Heidi. A Berlin magazine published an issue whose cover reproduced a painting by a young artist she knew and for whom she had sat. Its caption was 'The ideal Aryan girl'.

Meanwhile, the witch-hunt was raging in Berlin and a diligent bureaucrat discovered Heidi's grandfather's marriage licence, showing that her grandfather was Jewish. This was enough to cost Heidi's father his job. An eye surgeon, he was the head of a specialised clinic. The blow to a man deeply attached to his country was deadly. Crushed, he left Germany almost overnight for Chile.

Heidi's mother, completely unstrung by the course of events, crippled by a severe hip disability, which in any case made any travelling a serious problem, refused to accompany her husband, fearing it to be too much of a burden and also reluctant to leave her country and her only child.

The drama to which I tried in vain to suggest some solution, continued towards its climax. On one hand a desperate woman in Berlin, feeling abandoned, and on the other her only child in Paris, on the verge of a nervous breakdown, craftily master-minded by Guy. He knew all too well how to make my wife forget her responsibilities, promising her a glorious future with him thanks to the New Order, which would undoubtedly be established all over Europe. So Heidi neglected home and children, attracted by Guy's promises, pretending her mother's ordeal did not exist. Wanting to ignore her antecedents, which she wished were pure Aryan, she thought that the less she got in touch with her German family the better.

Incapable of coping with her own inner conflict, she gave way to neurasthenia, going from one doctor to another, from one psychiatric nursing-home to another, hoping to discover an escape that could only be found within herself.

Her mother, receiving only vague and dilatory answers to her anguished appeals from her beloved daughter, one evening yielded to the temptation of putting an end to it all. She committed suicide in her appartment by swallowing an overdose of sleeping pills. For Heidi this came as a terrible shock, from which she never completely recovered. Her subsequent behaviour must be understood as being the effect of a guilt complex which, although repressed, never lost its impact.

On returning home at the end of that afternoon in September 1938, this recent tragedy was in my mind. It had particularly affected me, as I held my mother-in-law in high esteem and my attempts to be helpful had never ceased.

Daladier's triumphant return had revealed the fragility of opposition against conquest and blind fanaticism, fomented on the other side of the Rhine. The future looked decidedly grim.

Before joining Heidi, whom I could hear moving about in her room, I automatically opened some letters that the janitor had handed me: one envelope was marked 'urgent' and my name was printed in block letters.

I read: 'Are you so credulous as to believe that the fair lady's charm alone is sufficient to make the degenerate descendant of a decadent nobility able to hypnotise a hussy more than ready to be taken in?'

The handwriting was disguised. There was no signature. A few spelling mistakes seemed done on purpose. Who was the writer? I tore it angrily to shreds. This did me good, but did not solve my immediate problem. How should I behave towards a woman whose instability was growing, and who pretended to go off in a fit whenever she felt like it, inaccessible to any sensible talk.

Some situations seem without solution. I was entangled in one of them. Heidi, whom I had not heard enter the room, started to accuse me of something. I knew immediately that the accusations she was hurling at me were a form of attack she favoured whenever she had taken a decision she thought I would fight.

'I'm quitting. For good. This very evening. I will let you have

6

my address. I'll return in a month to fetch the children. In the meanwhile you can have them. My place is not here.'

Worked up to a pitch of frenzy, she paid no heed to my protests.

A few minutes later, I heard the front door slam. A page in the book of my destiny had been turned.

I went to the window. Guy's Talbot was parked in front of the building. I saw her get into the car.

Poor Heidi, I could not help thinking. Poor, poor Heidi! She does not realise what she is doing!

I still cared for her, although in a detached way. Tenderness and a certain frustration at being unable to cope with her morbid condition can describe my state of mind.

2

Any disruption of family life creates an upheaval of which the children are sooner or later the victims.

As Zell, their Nanny, a nickname my elder daughter used for Mademoiselle, went on looking after the two girls, they did not immediately suffer from any emotional reaction.

Anne-Marie, the eldest, on whom the tension of recent months had left its mark, hid her thoughts behind a wall of silence. Martine, the youngest, whose health had been delicate since birth, required constant care. All this did not make Zell's task easy.

As the international situation worsened, I tried to speed up the divorce proceedings. More affected by my matrimonial misfortunes than I wished to acknowledge, I plunged feverishly into work, which left no time to think.

Memories of that hectic period are blurred; more so as the sharp outline of events one does not want to remember are quickly forgotten! Subsequently, less apparent circumstances may — to an awakened understanding, certainly will — reveal the logic of an unforeseen but inevitable sequence of facts. Due to this logic, every cause entails an effect, and transmits thereby the seed of new causes perpetuating the effects, unless they are dissolved by an understanding able to disrupt the chain. But, at that time I was far from realising that what I took for painful and most depressing facts would turn out to be a beneficial experience.

I remember that the night after Heidi's departure I burnt in an ashtray all her letters one by one, as well as a carefully preserved slip of paper on which I had written on the eve of our wedding, these meaningful words: 'Your decision is foolish, but you decided to marry Heidi with eyes wide open'.

I now know that certain bonds have to be tied even with the foresight that they will be severed later. This may be necessary to perceive behind what appears, that which appears not, in order to dissolve bonds forged in a past forgotten in the mists of time. Who can tell how fate works?

Days, weeks, and months went by. The phoney peace was followed by the phoney war, and then by the real war.

One day, on June 14th, the German motor-cycle spearhead roared into Paris. The occupation was beginning.

That morning, I was seated in a delivery-van loaded with crates crammed with documents.

Although people had deserted Paris in a panic-stricken exodus, I had remained at the plant I headed, working on technological projects for the Ministry of National Defence.

The suddenness of the German invasion had invalidated my determination to play an active part in a war, whose significance, in my mind, was greater than just a conflict among nations. As havoc reigned in the services of the Ministry, I suggested putting the incomplete prototype projects worked upon in different quarters in a safe place in Bordeaux.

I had also been asked to evacuate files that had been left behind in the Ministry of Internal Affairs, in order to save them from falling into the hands of the enemy.

There was no time to lose, and so at dawn on June 14th, I was sitting in a van beside Godot, an NCO previously assigned to the works located in the industrial outskirts of Paris. He was driving towards the Porte d'Orléans, one of the gates of the city, while the dull rumble of the motor cycles, preceding the bulk of the invading troops, could be heard in the near distance.

Aware that many bridges across the Loire had been destroyed, we expected to go a long way round to get to the South bank of the river. Luckily, we were able to carry a number of jerry cans filled with petrol.

I do not remember the roads we took, nor whether we found an undamaged bridge or whether we were ferried across the Loire. Anyway, we eventually succeeded in reaching Bordeaux, not without experiencing even in the areas spared by war that very special feeling given by the stillness preceding the storm, when, inert, but tense, nature seems to expect the impending unleashing of the elements.

We passed through apparently serene regions but we sensed intuitively that the population was in fact paralyzed by fear. The inhabitants were behaving strangely, their usual friendliness totally lacking. On the contrary they appeared to avoid us in a hostile manner.

On the way, we managed to make room in our crowded van for a few soldiers who had lost their units and thought they could find in Bordeaux — seat of the government at that period — authorities able to help them.

Among them was a British officer, anxious to embark either for England or for Africa. I don't know how he managed to get to the place where I picked him up, as he was reticent to tell us much about it. However, as I speak English fluently, we exchanged, at each stop, impressions on the world situation, the war, and the uncertain future. He declared that before the war he had commanded a regiment stationed in India but he did not give any details. As it was, we took a liking to each other. I was attracted by Dereck's dry humour, which helped to keep up our morale.

One evening, he confided:

'I am strongly influenced by Buddhism. While studying it, I discovered some long-forgotten Christian insights, and I am sure that if Europeans were converted to Buddhism they would cease their petty wargames.'

'You would lose your job!' I retorted jokingly.

'And so what? I would gladly become a monk. The Buddhist monks' yellow garb is just my style.'

Although spoken in jest, his words sounded sincere, the more so as he went on:

'To give up your usual background is a highly recommended exercise. Not knowing how to let go, we hang on to fictitious values and neglect those that are essential. The shattering of our background leads to progress, it gives us the chance and the ability to know ourselves, and is the only way to freedom.'

'It leads to progress?' I asked sceptically. 'My family background is shattered. I have left my old parents behind in a house at Corbeil, on the Seine, after having persuaded them to abandon their Paris home for fear of air-raids. Owing to the war situation, I reluctantly agreed to let my ex-wife take the children, although legally they are in my custody. I considered their physical safety in Biarritz more vital than contact with their mother's instability. And now the fighting is turning to disaster. You're telling me that all this leads to progress?'

Dereck, not in the least disconcerted, shook his head.

'No, not necessarily to progress, but to a good opportunity to enlarge the vision each of us has of the world. One must burst an abscess, and understanding the reasons which formed it enables one to uproot them.'

I interrupted.

'Uprooting solves nothing, it does not lead to anything concrete.'

Dereck shrugged his shoulders.

'Could you first explain the meaning of concrete or abstract? Are the dark forces at work nowadays, concrete? And are the forces opposing them, abstract? To join one camp or the other demands a choice. Having made that choice, when we arrive at the crossroads we possess the ability to fulfil our destiny. But we shall talk about all this some other time.'

On arrival at Bordeaux, our group scattered. Godot drove the loaded van to its destination, relieved to have succeeded in a difficult task, rendered more difficult by a broken axle, which had held us up only a hundred kms from our destination.

I deposited some documents at the bank. Then, eager for briefing, I went to the Prefecture Maritime in the hope of meeting my friend, Yvon, a naval officer. Fortunately, I found him.

'You're just in time', he exclaimed, when I was ushered in. 'I'm on the point of leaving this cursed city and its web of intrigues.'

'Where are you going?' I asked amazed. He lowered his voice.

'I am crossing the Channel. Why not join me?' His unexpected proposal confirmed my worse fears. The war was lost, at least on the Continent.

'Why not', I answered mechanically.

'Did you hear General de Gaulle's appeal?' insisted Yvon.

'No, what did he say?'

'He said that we had lost a battle, but not the war. Come along. A special branch of the Navy's Second Bureau will be set up in London. I am recruiting you.'

'To do what?' I was stirred by his enthusiasm.

'To return to France as soon as possible, in order to assemble in safe places all those unfortunate Czechs, Poles, Belgians and English who have been abandoned and are trapped in this country. During the coming weeks a lot will happen. Not all will go as may be wished. These men will have to be taken care of, saved from being sent to prison camps, and brought to us. They will be needed. Come along with me to London. We'll give you the means to do this job. You'll return, and as you speak German like a German and English like an Englishman, you will organise an escape route with its terminal in Great Britain. Do you get me?'

I did. The project sounded utopian, lacking any sound basis, inspired by wishful thinking just in the hope of preparing an immediate activity for the Naval Second Bureau. Neither Yvon nor I were aware that only a well thought-out plan could ensure the successful outcome of an operation fraught with risks. Nevertheless, the idea fired my enthusiasm. I again felt full of energy, ready for anything. I remembered what Dereck had said. Was this the way 'to know oneself'?

'Right. I'll come. When are you leaving?'

'Tomorrow, and so are you. Afterwards it may be too late. I'll see to all the arrangements.'

'You really want me to return to France right away?' I asked with sudden caution.

'Naturally, that is the main thing' confirmed Yvon.

'In that case, my two kids must not be left behind. It is too dangerous. If I were captured they would be hostages in the enemy's hands. For their sake I might be compelled to confess everything. It's unthinkable!'

Yvon scratched his chin.

'It's impossible to organise the evacuation of the children, unless . . . . . .'

'Unless?'

He looked at the calendar.

'Tomorrow evening a ship flying an Egyptian flag is stopping off in Sete to embark British subjects, officials, most of them stranded there . . . . . I shall sign a service order for you, give you a car and some petrol. Go and fetch your kids. You may embark with them. The Harbour Master of Sete is a friend. I'll phone him. He will do what has to be done. Okay?'

'But I would like to take Godot with me. He wants to go on with this war, and so does Dereck, an Englishman I met on the way.'

'That's your concern', said Yvon. 'Mine is to sign the service order, provide the vehicle and the petrol. The rest is up to you. Get going, time is short.'

He waved goodbye.

'We'll meet in London, at the Regent Palace Hotel. If I'm no longer there, the porter will have my address.'

I found myself again in the streets of this traffic-jammed city, in the throes of a feverish excitement. Rumours of all kinds were spreading. Confusion was everywhere.

Dereck and Godot were delighted at the prospect of escaping from hell's kitchen. The former, because it meant reaching home, the latter, because he thought it best to be guided by my decisions.

'Let's go, boss,' he rejoiced. 'We dash to Biarritz, carry off the kids and get out.'

Dereck was more level-headed.

'And what if their mother refuses?'

I had also been worrying about the possibility of Heidi's refusal. I only hoped I could see her alone and not in the presence of Guy or any other companion. I knew nothing of her undoubtedly hectic private life, but maybe time had made her more accessible to reason.

Speculation was useless. We would know the next day. That is what I told my two companions as we hurried off.

'Let's get the service order and the car. We'll fill the tank and a few jerrycans with gas and drive to Biarritz at dawn tomorrow. We must get cracking. It's quite a distance from Biarritz to Sete.'

And turning to Dereck, I asked jokingly:

'Is this unexpected drive across France pre-written in the history of my destiny?'

Dereck just smiled.

3

We arrived in Biarritz late that night and decided to wait until dawn before ringing the bell of Heidi's rented villa.

Dereck and Godot curled up on the back seat and fell into a restless sleep. Too nervous and keyed-up to do the same, I walked up and down the side street where we had parked the car.

My mind buzzed with conflicting thoughts. To take the children away was one part of the problem, to abandon their mother was another. Her unpredictable behaviour could not have been improved by her affair with Guy, a married man who — I thought — had no intention of leaving his wife, possessing the wealth he did not have. This affair could only result in a dead-lock, and its implications certainly endangered my future activities in France, particularly as I was sure that Germany would soon take over my country totally.

Moreover, I had reached the conclusion that it was Sylvie, Guy's wife, who, out of jealousy or for some other reason, had written or inspired the anonymous letter I had received on the memorable evening my wife had left me. To keep her husband, she could repeat this trick and this time the consequences might be far more serious.

Was I a Don Quixote tilting at windmills? Fears, hesitations, regrets, bitterness, alternated with exultant anticipation of a task, which I foresaw — perhaps to bolster up my courage — as heroic.

A world was collapsing under the weight of a power doctrine. Would I be crushed under the steam-roller?

Dereck, whom I had not heard approaching, grabbed my arm. And half jestingly, as usual, urged me to relax.

'To think clearly, you must be able to forget your rights. Accept your fate and let yourself be guided. The tension which has gripped you makes you forget today's urgent matters. See, the sky is growing pink. Let us storm the bulwark! Forward!'

14

And so the day of June 20th began. To say it was exhausting is an understatement.

I found Heidi in bed, fortunately alone. She did not wake up completely, as she was still under the influence of sleeping pills. As her resistance was apparently at its lowest ebb, I tackled her on the subject immediately.

'You think the children are a safeguard. You are wrong. I am certain that life in France will become extremely hard, more so because of your origin. You are risking getting involved in God knows what complications. I suggest you leave with us. I have decided to take the children, if necessary by force. Your affair with Guy will fizzle out. It is in your own interest to agree.'

'To go where?' she retorted, less reluctantly than I feared.

'To Africa or England, anywhere,' I answered evasively.

The argument dragged on for hours, until, shaken by my logic, she finally accepted.

Heidi, the children, Dereck, Godot and I left Biarritz late that morning. Before starting, I asked Zell to return to Paris as soon as possible with all Heidi's belongings which we could not take along. I gave her money, advised her to find my parents and tell them to return to their home and take care of her financially.

'Watch over my apartment in Neuilly', I said. 'We shall be returning soon.'

Zell agreed, frantically worried but without knowing our destination.

I shall never forget that drive from Biarritz to Sete. Heidi had fits of hysteria and even attempted to jump out of the car, one minute wishing to remain in France so as to join Guy, another to return to Berlin, or to keep her children, or to abandon them.

We reached Sete late at night. The Egyptian ship on which we were supposed to embark had just raised anchor, I heard from the Harbour Master, whom I got out of bed. Yvon had indeed phoned him. Although sympathising with my deep disappointment, he tried to make me give up my plan which he considered quite mad. He informed me of the latest news. The ship *Massilia* was not yet ready to sail and the members of

Parliament due to board her would not leave Bordeaux. The armistice would be signed — supreme insult — at Rethondes, the place of the signature of the German surrender in 1918. Marshal Pétain, sacrificing himself for his country, would remain in France.

'What's the use of persisting', he concluded. 'England is done for. She will give in within two weeks.'

I answered that I was certain she would not, telling him my reasons without convincing him.

'England will be the catalyst of the Free World' I stated. 'By the nature of things in this world, an imbalance must sooner or later be corrected. In time the Germans will regret their folly. Think of this when the time comes for you to choose sides.'

He shrugged his shoulders.

'It has come. I have chosen to obey the Marshal. Now, about helping you. I regret that there is nothing I can do. Except for the 'Pirates', a pair of unsavoury brothers, no possibility exists for getting out of here. The Pirates, that's what we call them, own the *Aurora*, sailing this decrepit vessel under the Panamanian flag. In a few hours, just before all sea traffic is halted, a stoppage which is due to happen at any moment now, the *Aurora* will leave Sete chartered by Belgian diamond merchants and their families. The payment was made in diamonds, the destination is Lisbon. The bosses — Peter and Costa — Greeks of the worst type, might agree to take you on board, thanks to certain methods of persuasion I can use, and thanks also to the money they will have no scruples in demanding. Look out for them at daybreak. Say I have sent you. And now, goodnight, it's two a.m. and I want to get some sleep.'

I returned slowly to the railway station, enjoying the fresh sea breeze. The night was beautiful. The stars were twinkling, the crickets were chirping. Nature was serene, and I too somehow felt at peace.

Sete station was bedlam. We had chosen it for our rallying point, but so had crowds of refugees. On the platform, Heidi and the two kids were sleeping on a make-shift bed of two luggage trolleys. Dereck and Godot were chatting quietly

16

among heaps of strange-looking luggage and ill-tied parcels; blankets were spread on the ground on which women and children were lying, waiting for any sort of transportation that would allow them to go further. Where to? They did not know. For them it was journey's end.

I told my two companions what I had learnt. Weariness subdued their reaction.

'Let's get some rest', suggested Dereck, 'and at daybreak we'll try, by united efforts, to get a favourable reply from Costa and Peter.' Then, paraphrasing a poster still covering the walls of French towns, he stated solemnly: 'We shall win, because we are the strongest!'

We eventually found the two Greeks sitting at a table in a café. They showed great reluctance, but agreed eventually to take us aboard the following hour. The fee they demanded proved unacceptable. To end the bargaining, I opened my wallet and drew out the money it contained.

'That's all I possess, take it or leave it. Our destination is Gibraltar, a port you can call at on your way.'

After a short discussion in their own language, they pocketed the money.

And so that morning began an appalling voyage. The *Aurora* fully deserved the qualification of 'decrepit old tub' conferred on her by the Sete Harbour Master. She was rusty, leaked, squeaked, pitched and rolled. The squalor and lack of comfort defied imagination.

We were packed together like sardines. Most of us were seasick. The food was uneatable. The children had to be content with bread softened in sweetened water and an occasional mug of condensed milk. The rest of us just tightened our belts and accepted what came with patience.

The Belgians were hostile, even offensive. They considered us intruders, particularly on account of Heidi, who being German, represented everything they were fleeing from. So we had to make do with the minimum available space. Dereck alone kept cheerful under the circumstances. He turned himself into a nanny, for Heidi, prostrate and exhilarated in turns, was more

17

interested in attracting Peter's attention than looking after the children. Out of lust, spite, defiance, or just wishing to escape the squalid promiscuity on board, she flung herself into his arms. Her behaviour certainly did not help matters.

Four days passed and I heaved a sigh of relief when we dropped anchor before Gibraltar, and a lighter approached the *Aurora*.

From then on Dereck became our guardian angel. Without his help, neither Heidi nor the kids could have disembarked. Thanks to his statement that he owed us his freedom, we were eventually allowed to do so.

Once again, Heidi tried to mess things up in a way which could have been amusing, but was actually pitiful.

At the very last minute, she declared she did not want to land, and suggesting letting me take the kids, wishing to make a new life with Peter. The latter, gesturing expressively behind her back, made me understand that he considered my wife's statement to be out of the question.

To imagine this ridiculous scene, it is necessary to realise that my two daughters and I were already in the lighter, tossed about by the swell, while Heidi still on board was shouting her proposals through a megaphone. The Belgians got aggressive and it was again Dereck who managed to make her see reason. She agreed to step down the gang ladder and join us. A few minutes later, we entered Gibraltar harbour.

We were lodged in an hotel where we could wash, rest and recover our mental balance. I was certainly in need of it. Fortunately, the British military wheels were well-oiled. The fortress authorities made the decisions for us. Dereck and I were to fly from Gibraltar to London. Godot would enlist with the French Free Forces, and later be sent to an assembly centre in Great Britain. Heidi and the children would embark on a cargo boat sailing in convoy to Liverpool.

I begged Heidi to be sensible, and for once, she was. I took leave of Godot who was sad at not being allowed to accompany me.

'As soon as I get to England, I'll look you up', he promised.

18

I did not tell him that my real intention was to leave England for the Continent as soon as possible. News spreads rapidly, and silence is golden, especially in wartime.

Two days later, we took off from Gibraltar airport.

After a five-hour flight, the green fields and pastures of England welcomed us. Happy and relieved, I quickly forgot the ordeals of the trip, ready for the next step.

4

I had entered another world. As I walked the streets of London, I could not help comparing the general atmosphere with the suffocating one of the Continent. Here, the inflexible determination of a besieged nation, conscious of a responsibility going beyond its immediate national interest: there, the prostration stemming from defeat, inducing — by reaction — an admiration for an apparently invincible war machine, in many minds justified by the lightning successes of a conqueror with whom it was undoubtedly wise to come to terms.

A good conscience, or its illusion, has always been a derivative to which men cling. That is why Marshal Pétain's policy was supported by such a large proportion of the French people. It veiled the true causes of defeat and did away with the individual or collective guilt complex of a nation unprepared for disaster.

As soon as the formalities with which foreigners escaping from the Continent had to comply had been fulfilled, I dashed to Stephen's house, the temporary headquarters of the Free French. Yvon welcomed me warmly and told me to enlist right away in the British Forces.

'You see', he said, 'the Naval Second Bureau is unable to introduce you into France, except by extremely risky means. We have as yet no logistic support. We are glad, on the other hand, to prove to the British that we have volunteers for operations enabling us to infiltrate into enemy occupied territory so as to establish communications over there. Admiral Muselier, heading the Second Bureau, is in full agreement. Moreover, you hold a major asset: your travelling companion, Dereck, is one of the top brass of the military branch of the Intelligence Service. If you have made up your mind, you can soon be in Marseille. Muselier will provide you with absolutely reliable local contacts. His friends, former Marines, are devoted to him, and are eagerly awaiting a chance to get into harness again. It'll be a piece of cake!'

I saw no reason why I should not accept his proposal as it seemed quite sound. I was totally unaware of the under-currents agitating the different factions around the chiefs of Free France, those having reached London wanting to assert their authority towards both the British and their own com-patriots.

The four weeks in England passed quickly. I enlisted for the duration of the war and joined the military section of the Service, which from now on would guide my steps and take all necessary measures for the children's safety and welfare.

Heidi would know nothing of my whereabouts. She would be told that I had been sent to South Africa, which would anyhow be my official destination. As the fear of infiltrated spies was at its height, I was asked to refrain from talking about my mission and also from meeting friends in French circles. If the enemy got to know about my stay in England, it would put me in mortal danger on the Continent.

Heidi would be given an apartment in a residential area in London; she would be free to come and go as she pleased, and see her daughters whenever she wished. They would be en-trusted on arrival to a family with children of the same age, living in West Drayton. However, she would not have the right to take the children away.

As to my future identity, we agreed to use the passport of a refugee from Brittany, after of course changing the photo-graph.

'It is safer, at least for the immediate future', declared the officer in charge of organizing my mission in close co-operation with Yvon. 'Real papers', he went on, 'are much better than forged ones. And Brittany is far from the South of France where you will be operating. Now here is your plan of action.'

Seated behind his desk, he offered me a cigarette. I took it but did not light it. I needed to concentrate on the instructions that were about to be given to me.

'First, you will be flown to Lisbon. There, you will go to the Vichy Embassy to request a pass for your repatriation through Spain. You will not be the only one. All civil servants from here and elsewhere who have chosen Vichy have to go through the same procedure. You will succeed because the newly-appointed officials of the Vichy France embassy have no means of control and no time for checking. Once in Marseille, you'll go underground. Yvon will provide you with a list of marines believed to be on our side. The pass-word is Youki, the name of Admiral Muselier's dog, an animal well known to those he once commanded. You will correspond to us through Rhea. I will give you her address in Lisbon. You will send her passionate love-letters and your reports, in invisible ink, will be written between the lines. I'll give you the ink recipe which you will prepare yourself with ingredients easy to find on the spot. Later on, we'll send you a 'pianist', a wireless operator and his transmitter. Meanwhile, you'll have to manage on your own.'

I nodded.

'But tell me', I asked him, 'how am I going to track down the English, Poles, Czechs, Belgians and even French who may want to get to England? They will certainly not be recognisable at first sight.'

'If I knew', he said wearily, 'I'd go and fetch them myself. You'll just have to use your wits.'

The interview was over. I stayed behind in the small office of this apparently innocuous building in the middle of London and went to the window.

'Look at this street, at the cars and passers-by', I mused.

'The Adventure with a capital A has begun. Its outcome will be fatal. Realise it while you are still alive. Question yourself:

'Are you ready for it?'

'No', replied my fear.

'Give it up', advised my reason.

'Never', answered a voice from the depths of my inner self.

A few days later, I left for Liverpool to fetch Heidi and the children. I took the two little girls to the home of Nancy and John in West Drayton, while Heidi moved into her London flat. Everything was now under control and all I had to do was to wait.

I explained to Nancy why my daughters should not be taken away by their mother. She understood the situation immediately and seemed delighted to increase her family, thereby allowing the 'Frenchie' — that was I — to do his patriotic duty.

Heidi seemed satisfied, as almost all of my officer's pay had been allotted to her. I suggested she looked for a job, and although she agreed, I learnt later that she never did so.

The parting from my daughters was very difficult.

'I'll be seeing you soon', I told them, knowing that 'soon' might well be 'never'. Martine was crying, while Anne-Marie watched me stony-faced, unable to imagine her new life amid total strangers, whose language she did not understand. I shall never forget the vision of the little girl with her two neat braids, standing motionless, petrified by grief. It was indeed a heartbreaking moment.

On the eve of my departure, I had a long talk with Dereck.

Against his habit, he spoke very warmly:

'Be lighthearted. By making your choice, you have joined a higher order, an order far beyond personal or national consideration, an order of a spiritual nature. From now on, you will not be alone.'

The following day at five a.m. I left my room in a building near Westminster Abbey and climbed into a taxi sent by the

Service. The driver was under orders to take me to an airport near London, without stopping even in the event of an air-raid alarm.

No sooner had we started than waves of German bombers approached the city. The anti-aircraft guns were blazing, the ground shook from explosions, and the unceasing humming of planes was heard in the distance. The streets were empty; the sinister wailing sirens had driven everybody into shelter. A few shrill whistles here and there revealed the presence of the Home Guard. The war had finally struck London.

The day before, walking in the streets, I had seen these men in uniform with sticks as their only weapons. Guns were scarce since Dunkirk. Nevertheless, one of them cheerfully said, having noticed my astonished look:

'If the Jerries invade us, each inhabitant of these Isles will kill at least one. We are forty-five million men, women and children. So you can be sure that the whole Wehrmacht will be wiped out.'

His calm assurance left me speechless. Did he even begin to know what Britain was up against?

The taxi was moving slowly as the explosions were getting closer and gaining in intensity. The yellow and red flames of fires mingled with the hues of dawn darkened by smoke.

Suddenly, about two hundred yards away, a wall collapsed, blocking the street ahead, while the blast of the explosion threw the cab off its course. The driver calmly stopped. He took his cap off his head, replacing it by a steel helmet.

'Sorry', he said, turning round, quite unconcerned. 'The road's blocked. We'll have to make a detour. Too bad, but that's war!'

Shaken by the turmoil around me, and heading into the unknown, I whole-heartedly admired this extraordinary self control.

Fear had kept France behind the Maginot Line; fear had paralysed every initiative; fear had led to successive surrenders and, finally, total collapse. It was fear that had propelled millions of people on to the roads of France.

The driver's gesture at that particular moment had a symbolic value.

'We'll win the war', I cried inwardly, and that certainty never left me. It was this which helped me to convince my friends in the Resistance that we would win. Faith moves mountains, and faith helped me in my most difficult moments.

At the airport, Yvon and the officer I had met at the Service joined me to make sure that the customs and identity controls would offer no difficulty. I was supposed to be a diplomat being repatriated via Lisbon, and no apparent favour had to be extended to me.

'Farewell', said Yvon. 'And Good Luck!'

The officer winked while pointing discreetly towards a couple standing with their backs turned, next to me.

'Don't trust them', he whispered. 'They're Bulgarians. Their name is Borzareff. Bulgaria is an ally of the Rome-Berlin Axis.'

We took off. A few hours later, Lisbon appeared under the wing of our plane which still displayed its Dutch markings, a civilian plane that had chosen freedom at the time of the German invasion.

Lisbon, unconcerned, old-fashioned, carefree, gave the illusion of having succeeded in stopping the march of time. The people were enjoying themselves. Maybe the laughter of numerous refugees, happy to have reached this haven, rang false, but nothing recalled the war-torn Continent.

In the evening, the city sparkled with light, an even greater contrast to London's total blackout. And the sumptuous Colonial Exhibition dazzled my eyes.

I was strolling around with the Borzareffs; in spite of the warning I could not help liking them. Maybe Tania had something to do with the pleasure I felt, walking at her side, admiring the splendid monuments built for the Exhibition.

We decided to have dinner together. Exotic dishes, heady wines, bright lights, the crowd in its Sunday best, blurred the image stamped on my mind of a wall collapsing. Where? Elsewhere. When? This morning!

An unbearable contrast between the convulsions of the world and the apparent unconcern of a neutral city.

The next morning I called on the French Embassy, and a day later, provided with the necessary papers, I boarded a train for Madrid.

The peaceful Portuguese scenery went past our coach window, till we reached Valencia de Alcantara, the frontier post on the Spanish side.

All the passengers alighted for passport control. When my turn came, the inspector curtly informed me that new regulations forbade the passage of French nationals into Franco's Spain.

'I'll return your passport tomorrow morning on arrival of the train at Lisbon', he concluded. 'You must return.'

So my passage through Spain was blocked. I was at a total loss. What next? I paced the station platform now deserted, and stopped in front of a poster bearing the Phalangist sign. Arrows joined in the centre were aiming their darts towards the sky. Were they going to pierce me?

A voice made me turn round.

'Pobre Frances!'

A young girl with very dark eyes and hair was addressing me.

'Pobre Frances!'

I had noticed her before, leaning against the railings running along the platform.

'Come with me', she invited, waving her hands. I was only too happy to accept, and together we left the station.

I tried to take her arm but she slipped away, smiling: 'My fiancé alone has this right'. She underlined each word by gestures, seeing that my knowledge of Spanish was limited.

'Follow me! I'll take you to my parents.'

5

Pedra led me along quickly, talking fast, quite forgetting that the 'pobre frances' knew only the rudiments of her own language.

At a short distance from the station, we entered a small grocer's shop on the ground floor of a dilapidated house, the shelves of which were filled with a strange medley of empty tins for the benefit of customers conspicuously absent. A stale, foul smell struck my nostrils, a smell of cinammon, mustard, wet jute, cheese and fish, probably impregnated for years in the wooden counter and shelves.

The father — a stocky man with a wooden face — was standing behind the counter. The mother, a kerchief over her head, was peeling vegetables at the back of the shop.

Pedra explained how she had met me. I caught the words: 'pobre frances, passaporte, policia, su madre'.

On the way, I had managed to tell her that I was most upset at having to give up my journey, as I was very worried about my mother's poor health.

I tried to complete my limited Spanish vocabulary with Latin words to which I gave a Spanish twist. And this jargon helped me to make myself understood, especially as I improved it little by little.

Pedra's father listened impassively until his daughter's flow of words petered out. He then extended his hand, his eyes reflecting a certain curiosity and some suspicion.

'You are at home and my house is yours', he said finally, with a courtesy worthy of a Spanish grandee. I noticed Pedra's relief at this greeting, and with a delighted smile she immediately took me to a kind of shed opening on to a tiny garden equipped with a water pump. She told me that I could have a wash if I so wished and left, but returned with a mattress which she spread on the floor. A little later, she came back to ask me to join the family for the evening meal.

The shed reeked of the same smell as the shop but even more intensly. My head ached badly and a feeling of utter helplessness overcame me.

What should I do? To whom could I turn? Nobody, nowhere, need worry about my fate. I did not exist, I was just a ghost holding a passport without a Portuguese entry visa, since the one issued in London was for transit only and was therefore no longer valid. Spain was expelling me. Portugal refused to let me in. How could I get out of this mess?

Two days before, while walking around Lisbon, I had to my surprise caught sight of the *Aurora,* at anchor in port. Playing the curious tourist, I questioned an English-speaking sailor sitting on a bollard. He explained volubly that it was a ship carrying Jews without a visa. They were waiting for permission to disembark, but would do well to clear out.

'There are already enough refugees in Lisbon. We don't need them or anybody else', was his final remark, and he spat on the ground to emphasise his views, probably shared by his country's authorities.

Tense and sorry for myself I joined the family who had so spontaneously offered to shelter a foreigner in distress. My face clearly reflected my state of mind, and I learnt that this had been a major factor in a vital decision, decisive for what was to come.

Pedra's brother, José, a chap of about thirty, with a low forehead and gleaming eyes, watched me intently throughout the simple meal served by the mother with her daughter's help.

We ate in silence. Tension relaxed at the appearance of a bottle of red wine. We clinked glasses and José began to cross-examine me.

'Who was I?' 'Where did I come from?' 'Where was I going?' 'What was my opinion of the war in general and of the Civil War, which had just ceased, in particular?'

On my guard, trying to act the part of my borrowed identity, Henri Jonquière, I replied:

'The German advance drove me out of the factory where I was working as a foreman on a special assignment. As I believed the war would go on, I fled to Lisbon hoping to embark for

Africa. However it fizzled out, and now I want to get back to my native Brittany to see my sick mother, if she is still alive. As for the war, it is a dreadful business.'

After that statement, the father intervened — until then he had just listened.

'What is your attitude towards Fascism and what will it be in your country?' he asked.

Did the question conceal a trap? Mechanically I looked at Pedra and saw encouragement in her eyes.

'I'll fight against it with all my strength!' I replied.

Pedra's smile rewarded me. After a pause José smiled too.

'I'm leaving tomorrow morning to visit Pedra's fiancé. He is a good friend of mine. He thinks and acts the right way. You may come with me. I know how to avoid check-points.'

He spoke slowly, with gestures making sure I understood his proposal.

Taken aback, I nodded and anxiously asked: 'And from there?' José shrugged his shoulders as if deploring my naïve question.

'You will be guided of course from friend to friend until you reach France. 'They' won, but 'we' are carrying on the war in a different way. Get me?'

I did. His words dispelled my hesitation.

'I must get my passport back. It's essential in case of trouble.'

'There will be no trouble,' José asserted. 'You'll get it back. The Inspector will return it tomorrow, when you board the eleven o'clock train from Madrid to Lisbon. Get into the rear coach. A few minutes after the train starts, jump out. It will be moving slowly on a sharp turn. I'll be waiting with your suitcase in a cornfield on the right side of the track. That's all you have to do. I'll see to the rest.'

That night I hardly slept. Leaning against the wall of the shed, I gazed up at the stars and my thoughts wandered from my kids to Paris and to a bygone world that existed only in memory.

Gradually, a feeling of detachment overcame me. I imagined that this was how I would feel when my soul was ready to leave my body.

Daybreak came at last. Pedra brought me a warm drink and chatted gaily in an attempt to cheer me up, but without much success.

After having thanked her parents for their spontaneous kindness, Pedra and I left for the station. I had to wait a long time for the train. Finally I got into the rear coach. The same Inspector, who had taken it the previous day, returned my passport. I waved discreetly to Pedra. A few minutes after the train's departure, I jumped on to the track and disappeared into a field where the tall cornstalks hid me from sight.

José whistled. I joined him, we shook hands and left together across the fields. After a long walk, we finally arrived at a small town. It was market-day. A rickety old bus was parked near a square crowded with market-stalls doing hectic business. José waved a friendly greeting to the driver and we got in. The clandestine crossing into Spain had begun.

I disposed of money hidden in the false bottom of my suitcase which the Service had provided: French banknotes, pesetas and dollars. I was therefore able to reimburse my escorts for the expenses they incurred, although they never asked for a cent.

Today, thinking it over, I can better understand the reasons which had induced José and all those who, like him, willingly helped someone like me, in spite of the risks they ran.

The end of the Civil War had settled nothing. The loser's resentment was still vivid, and underground action distils a subtle poison which I, too, was to taste. This poison has the power to split your personality in two: your own and a second one beyond, giving a feeling as intoxicating as that produced by a potent drug, a feeling of floating high above the mass of mankind. To experience this, you have to plunge into the underground, even if it means inventing the means of doing it.

The Spaniard is too proud to accept defeat easily. He tends to adopt and devote himself entirely to a particular cause, with a mystical rather than a political idealism. And he will serve this cause unswervingly, even if it means defying superior forces.

For four years I was in contact with men who risked their lives as guides or escorts. There is no need to point out that clandestine action, whatever its form, is only possible when based on full knowledge of the geography and customs of the country, of its police — at the time still unorganized — and on the support of friends and relatives.

We progressed through Spain by varied means, including mule-drawn carts, trains, and even a private car, lent by an obliging driver, without the owner's permission, as well as by buses.

Information on check-points, police patrols, danger spots, was never lacking, and I had the impression that my escorts enjoyed this game of hide-and-seek.

Undoubtedly, people who play this game must be as much at home in the country as a fish in water. It is an axiom as old as the hills. Only a person absolutely familiar with a particular area can find his way about easily and confidently.

We stayed overnight with the people of the localities we were in, in coal miners' cottages, barns and church vestries. Everything went off without a hitch. Except, however, on one occasion, when things failed to go according to plan.

We had by now crossed the Estramadoura and New Castille provinces and had reached Aragon. The peaks of the Pyrenees loomed on the horizon, and I realised that France was within reach.

That day, a mule-cart was our vehicle. The escort, a boy, Pedro, bubbling over with vitality, had just been released from a camp where the victors had imprisoned the defeated, although they wore the same uniform. We saw during our trip these beaten soldiers, crushing stones on the roads, guarded by armed Moors. When we passed, they looked up dully, arousing our compassion. It was a pitiful sight and traces of that fratricidal war could be seen everywhere: gaping trenches, destroyed houses, starving, ragged children. We skirted round the large cities, some of them in ruins. However, I could still see far worse poverty there than in the countryside.

Pedro suddenly decided to visit his girl friend who lived in a farm along our route. He asked his brother-in-law, the cart-driver to stop, and got off near a town whose citadel was visible in the distance.

'You will leave the cart when you reach a small wood just ahead. Keep away from the road, hide and wait for the night,' he instructed me. 'Don't forget that in Spain people go to bed late. At about two a.m, there is no risk. Enter the town, go beyond the cathedral in the direction of the citadel, walk up the street. A few yards from the square on the right there is a *bodega*. My brother's house is just opposite.'

He scribbled a plan on a piece of paper and handed it to me.

'You can't miss it. The green door has a hammer-shaped knocker. Give two sharp taps and two others after an interval. My brother is expecting me and will open the door. Tell him I am with Carmen and that I'll come tomorrow. He will understand and give you lodgings. *Adios!*'

He jumped out of the cart and disappeared behind the curve of a field. The brother-in-law cracked his whip and the mules trotted off.

At two a.m. I knocked at Pedro's brother's house. Nobody answered. I kept drumming the indicated rhythm, but the door remained closed. Afraid of arousing the neighbours, and disheartened, I decided to give up. I returned to the square I had just crossed. Foot-sore after a journey of three weeks which had included walking and climbing in mountainous areas, I stumbled along the cobbled road until I caught sight of a faint light and instinctively went towards it. The night was not dark, stars were shining, the air was invigorating, but my only thought was to find a place to rest in until dawn. To be caught by the police so near my goal would have been heart-breaking.

Light shone from two glass globes, one ruby-red and the other emerald-green, placed in a shop window surmounted by a sign on which the word *Farmacia* stood out in gold letters. I climbed the two steps leading to the entrance, and, astounded by my own boldness, firmly turned the ball-shaped handle. The door opened and I entered the pharmacy while a bell tinkled overhead.

What on earth are you doing in this place? I asked myself, on the point of turning round and tip-toeing away.

A voice stopped me. *'Cerrado la puerta'*. 'Close the door.'

31

The gentle tone and the simple words were astounding under the circumstances. Where could I go?

The man who had spoken was short. Very short. He reminded me of a gnome straight out of the fairy-tales that had delighted my childhood. He was standing in front of a lectern, his head the height of the tilted board, his eyes hidden behind thick glasses. His face almost touched the sheet of paper on which he was writing. Between each sentence, he raised his pen to his lips, apparently deep in thought, while he moved his head, crowned by a mop of grey hair, to the left and to the right. I had plenty of time to observe him. My arrival did not appear to interrupt his work in which he seemed totally absorbed.

I dared not move for fear of disturbing him. A green lamp-shade fixed on the lectern was projecting a cone of light. It took me a few minutes to realise that he was not writing. He was composing, inwardly listening to music only he could hear.

Dead-tired, I sat down as quietly as possible on a high stool near the railing separating the room into two equal parts, the one we were in, the other apparently reserved for dispensing.

Shelves stocked with fat-bellied pots bearing strange inscriptions covered most of the wall, a spicy fragrance filled the air. In vain I tried to keep my eyes open, and leaning my head against the railing, I dozed off.

A voice suddenly aroused me. I jumped to my feet and, forgetting where I was, mumbled an apology in French.

The gnome looked at me kindly. The eyes behind the strong lenses seemed abnormally large.

'We'll talk tomorrow. You are obviously at the end of your tether. Lie down on this couch. After resting, you can explain the reason of your late visit.'

As he spoke, he led me to a recess adjoining the room. I fell on the couch, dead to the world.

6

I woke up without suspecting that the days spent in Jaca would mark a turning point in my life. Only when remembering them much later in their true perspective did I realise the significance of a particular approach to essential problems of life, which Garcia revealed to me. Subsequently I had the opportunity and the good fortune to enlarge my understanding of these essential questions, thereby changing my vision of the world.

My first impression was that my host had come straight out of a fairy-tale. When he stepped down from his room to meet me, I almost expected he would turn the pharmacy into a goblin castle.

As he stood by the couch on which I had spent the night, he gave the impression of having the body of a lanky child with a prematurely aged head. His wrinkled face shone with great kindness. His unusually strong lenses added to his strange appearance. In short, he was unlike anybody I had ever met.

I did not know where I was. I had already decided not to ask my different escorts even the most ordinary questions about our itinerary, so as to avoid any suspicion of mistrust.

My host introduced himself as Garcia. Then he asked me what business had brought me to Jaca. I was unable to find a satisfactory or even a plausible answer to this natural question. The only possibility was to tell part of the truth. So I confessed having entered and crossed Spain illegally with the help of friends. However, I did insist that my beloved mother's illness had compelled me to break the law, hoping to be able to see her before she passed away.

Garcia had a very astute mind. I realised this only later. He did not interrupt me, but I felt he did not believe me.

Finally, I suggested that if he felt he ought to, he should do his duty and hand me over to the police.

Smiling enigmatically he invited me to share his breakfast. He offered me a slice of corn bread, poured some substitute

33

coffee into cups, handed me one, and peering at me short-sightedly through his thick glasses, addressed me abruptly, but courteously.

'You are not telling me the whole truth. Your sick mother is not a sufficient reason for risking imprisonment in a concentration camp in my beautiful country. You are neither a black-marketeer, nor an anarchist, nor an adventurer. I can easily evaluate whoever I speak to. However, I have no desire to force your confidence. I am now going to see the owner of the house with the green door which you told me about. He must be very frightened, particularly if his brother, Pedro, has joined him. Fear is a bad counsellor. Do not show yourself outside this room. Today is Sunday, the pharmacy is closed, and nobody will disturb you. On my return, we'll decide what to do.'

Deeply affected, I was unable to utter a word. My eyes dimmed with tears. Apprehension concerning my situation had grown steadily, and the idea of imprisonment putting an end to my endeavours was distressing. Hope gave me a new sense to life.

Finally, I managed to stammer:

'You're quite right. I did not tell you the whole truth. But I'll complete my story later.'

I did, and never regretted it. Not only did Garcia introduce me to an unsuspected universe, not only did I — thanks to him — take a glimpse into an unknown dimension of our world, but he also became a most precious collaborator. After the German occupation of the Southern half of France, his house was permanently used as a halting place in the trans-Pyrenees escape route to Gibraltar.

Garcia was of Basque origin. After living for many years in the Basque province of France, he returned to Spain and had chosen Jaca — a charming little hillside town and holiday resort — to carry on his researches into the secrets of Alchemy.

Jaca, he informed me, was an important turntable on the way to Compostella, the route taken by the Alchemists in their quest for wisdom. 'This route' he added, 'is strewn with untouched vestiges of the past. It is not only by chance that it was named

34

the Road of the Stars, the path leading to the secrets of the universe. Compostella, if rightly understood, leads to Mastership and defines the object of the great alchemical work. I have been searching in nearby caves for revealing inscriptions. The Civil War interrupted my work. Were I to resume it now, I would risk trouble from ignorant bureaucrats. This is why I am willing to support a cause that will re-establish — let us hope — the possibility for everyone to evolve freely. I believe that chance is merely a law which — like yourself — travels incognito. If the green light led your steps to me, there was a reason for it. Nature is green and so is emerald, a stone which I particularly value. That is why I changed the traditional blue pharmacy light to emerald green.'

I listened but did not really understand. My scepticism told me that some of his statements were just a harmless fantasy.

One evening, I asked Garcia to tell me the significance of the stuffed salamander cemented into the middle of the pharmacy ceiling. The beast gave the impression of swooping head downwards upon the customers. My enquiry made him laugh, a noiseless laugh characteristic of him.

'My customers,' he finally replied, 'notice only what is under their noses. If they were to raise their heads, their bewilderment would make them ask silly questions. So they prefer to keep silent, and remain ignorant of what is essential, never looking beyond their noses.'

Some hidden impulse made me control my curiosity, but I did not reject his words as irrational. He gazed at me for a long time and I felt the magnetism of his eyes, enlarged by his glasses. It left me numb, and I did not move until he went on:

'Have you given a thought to the fact that subtle energies provide cohesion to all things? Stone, metal, plants, animals, man, are penetrated by fluidic radiance to which the cells, both of inert and living matter are tuned. This 'tuning' supplies the cells with information which determines their behaviour and their respective specificity. If a metal rod breaks, the molecules rush to the damaged part as if to strengthen it. The cells in our body hasten to close an opening caused by a wound. Do you follow me?'

I nodded.

'To understand the laws commanding those energies, to enable man to direct his vital influx, so as to replace an instinctive action by a deliberate action, guided by intelligence, makes all the difference. The true meaning of intelligence is to know that it must seek a reality veiled by visible phenomena and to behave accordingly' He paused: 'Does this seem logical to you?'

I nodded again.

'Then you should be aware that such cognition does not just happen. It can only develop thanks to an inner silence transforming egocentric willpower into an availability of the heart and the soul. To be actively available, one has to abandon one's habits, even of thought. One has to learn to forget one's desires, however normal they may be. To be available means to be free from the ego in order to become an impassive spectator of whatever action is needed at that very moment, regardless of whether it leads to victory or defeat.'

He turned his gleaming eyes upon me. Once more the force of his magnetism hit me like a sudden flash, leaving me speechless.

'I will teach you some exercises to help you discover what is hidden behind the façade of what we normally perceive. You will need all your wits. You must learn to be calm in action and to be active in calmness. As you knocked at my door, you were guided to do just that. Consequently, it is my wish to answer your quest. It will be my contribution to the effort to halt the present outburst of violence.'

I listened, not knowing what to think. Much later I was able to understand how seemingly accidental encounters occur, which, if recognised, enable one to act beyond all personal considerations.

A strange atmosphere prevailed during our talks. Garcia's rapid gait and his alertness in answering my questions disconcerted me. He dressed with care, wearing loose clothes. His unruly hair was turning grey and he liked to pace up and down his long narrow laboratory, his hands clasped behind his back. This room opened on to a courtyard surrounded by a wall, which screened us from indiscreet eyes.

He received his customers in the pharmacy. The tinkle of the bell over the entrance door announced them and interrupted our talks from time to time. The potions and infusions, compounded lovingly, were heated on a wood-fire on the hearth, located in the far end of the laboratory. Retorts and a number of big-bellied stoneware jars, some labelled, some not, were lined up on racks. He fondled them with his rather short-fingered hands, before producing various dried herbs and other ingredients.

I should have liked to show my host my gratitude but I did not know how. Thus — I thought — the best I could do was to listen attentively to his words even if they seemed to have but a remote relation to my immediate problems.

It is only now, years later that I realised the importance of his teaching, which he considered to be his true mission. Of that I only became aware long after we had parted.

'You cannot', he stated the day following my arrival, 'act with Cartesian logic in an unbalanced world. From a logical viewpoint the adventure you now commit yourself to is rushing you into the lion's mouth. It can end only in the bathtub with your head being kept under water by some Gestapo swine, unless you understand that in order to prevent such a fate you have to abandon your intellectual approach. In every man certain faculties lie dormant which, if awakened, enable him to pick up messages emanating from superior worlds. These will guide and preserve him from impulsive action.'

'Superior worlds?' I asked, quite bewildered.

'Precisely', he answered, not in the least disconcerted. 'Nevertheless, there is a rule which says that no secret shall be confided to those not yet qualified to receive it. As far as I can see, you are *not* prepared and my responsibility is therefore immense. There are only two possibilities: either you are unable to understand and so I would be speaking in vain, or you will act without conviction, experiencing failure and becoming discouraged.' He paused a few seconds.

'All the same, I shall initiate you!'

'What is the reason that drives you?' I broke in timidly. It took some time for the answer.

'You were able to forget yourself in order to embrace a cause beyond the usual national or political reasons. Circumstances have obviously fostered your decision, but I am convinced that if your steps have led you to me, certain facts account for it.

'Freedom, as Goethe said, is the essence of Spirit. Freedom must be preserved. Without it, anything we stand for is jeopardised. Alchemy is the science of transformations induced by Light, the Light of Spirit. The world is an Athanor, an alchemistic oven, and we humans are here to ensure that the 'cooking' is carried out according to the Law of Life and not against it.'

'And what is this law?'

He shrugged his shoulders.

'It is of no consequence. It is impossible in a few hours to introduce you into the arcana of an ancestral tradition. Follow my instructions. They will help to free you from fear, and only those who know how to pass beyond fear, only those who know how to rise above conflict, only those who know how to forget themselves, have a chance to stay alive in a universe ruled by men who have let loose the whirlwind without knowing the master word which would quell it.'

During the next few days, Garcia made pertinent suggestions regarding many aspects of correct action, and he advised me to remember them. I promised I would, but more to please him than out of conviction. Subsequently I had the opportunity to put these suggestions into practice and found them invaluable. In fact, they changed the course of my life and greatly contributed towards shaking my former belief that only the tangible world had any reality.

After a short week, Pedro, whom my host had met the day following my arrival and who had stayed on at his brother's home, came to fetch me at nightfall. We walked, or rather climbed, through woods and finally reached a railway station at daybreak. An engine and its tender were halted at a siding. Pedro ordered me to climb into the tender, under the watchful eye of a taciturn engine-driver, who made my hiding place safe by piling coal and heavy logs around it.

The convoy, consisting of the engine, tender and one coach, started after a long delay. In such a situation the seconds drop one by one and the slow passing of time is liable to produce panic with all its disastrous effects.

Eventually the train steamed through tunnels, ascended slowly, stopped frequently and finally arrived at a border station by the entrance of a tunnel, the last halt on the soil of the Iberian peninsula.

At the other end of the tunnel lay France! The driver shunted his train into the tunnel where he slowed down to let me extricate myself from my hiding place and jump off the tender. Without losing a second, he backed out.

According to Pedro's instructions, I did not hesitate and resolutely walked along the track to the French end of the tunnel, which I perceived far ahead. When I reached it, I ran right into two gendarmes whom, to their great amazement, I embraced.

I do not remember what I told them. They showed their sympathy in asking me to have a drink with them, and so ended an unforeseen adventure. That same evening I was in a train bound for Marseille with a valid ticket in my pocket.

Gratefully I breathed the rank odours of the over-crowded coaches. We were packed together, but I was thankful to be on a French train once more.

7

To comprehend the hectic atmosphere then prevailing in Marseille, it is necessary to recall the events of the summer and autumn 1940.

Russia controlled the Baltic States, Germany had swept through the Balkans, Italy had attacked Greece, and in the foreground of this struggle for influence, there were tragic confrontations of Mers-el-Kebir and Dakar during which Free French vessels shelled other French vessels.

In France, Laval's rise to power, the promulgation of the Constitutional Acts and the series of decrees designed to set up the New Order, deeply upset public opinion, ill-prepared for such drastic changes.

Marseille, Phoenician city, was the microcosm of a world falling apart; it offered the observer a varying aspect of hope and despair; alternating, as if produced by a kaleidoscope, the contradictory shades and trends generated by upheavals never experienced before.

Public reaction fluctuated according to the sensational news whispered or spread in many ways, and often meant to confuse. Newspaper headlines publicised the German communiques, announcing England's destruction by air-raids, emphasising the heavy losses incurred at sea, and underlining the Jewish-Freemason domination of the rest of the world.

From October onwards, Mussolini's march on Athens was not making much headway. The newspaper vendors invented jeering headlines, as for instance: 'Spaghetti eaters stuffed in grease!' (Greece).

On my arrival at the Saint Charles railway station, I was entering a keyed-up city whose population had doubled since the exodus from other parts of France.

Only gradually I became aware of the currents and cross-currents creating a constant tension which affected everybody.

Exceptional circumstances incline man to self-preservation,

trying either to just survive or else to take advantage of the situation to make easy money out of the despair of others.

The people of Marseille have always been resourceful. The Black Market got under way and the underworld quickly took over, but, not however in haste, in order to avoid mistakes. They well knew that sooner or later they would be asked to collaborate with the victors; police forces throughout the world require stooges and informers.

The oldest profession in the world can also be used as an ideal observation post. The 'customer' readily loses his reserve with his female choice of the moment, particularly if the woman partner knows how to appeal to his sensitivity.

Most refugees were totally uprooted. France was cut in two, and any return to the Occupied Zone was momentarily impossible. It was equally impossible to leave the national territory unless powerful connections could be set in motion.

Therefore, trapped in the city, those who had money gathered at the aperitif hour in the various places chosen by different groups, drifting together according to former or present political sympathies.

The fashionable bar Cintra was the local centre for Vichy supporters. The world of finance, of show business, and those trying on the fringe of high society to collect some crumbs which may have been overlooked, discussed the situation as they wished to see it.

Observers from the two Axis countries — Germany and Italy, listened in, as well as the more or less secret agents of both countries.

Over drinks, pros and cons were hotly discussed, but to show confidence in the part France had to play in the New Order, it was generally insisted against all evidence that the war should soon be over.

Elsewhere, opinions differed. They wavered between faith in Pétain, the victor of Verdun, and the shock caused by defeat, between the wish to see France as a referee, and the bitter disappointment that helplessness breeds.

In yet other places, in lowly pubs, those who had lost

everything lived from day to day, and remained silent.

Men walked the streets from morning to night in search of a job, returning hopeless, while their anxious wives waited, knowing the search must be in vain.

In the sultry streets of the Old Harbour, the brothels displayed Full House notices, as the flow of patrons ebbed only in the early hours of the morning. The choice was greater than usual as women, driven by hunger, resorted to prostitution.

Such was Marseille!

Since all the hotels were full, I wandered through the streets in search of a lodging. A moan startled me. I walked towards where it came from and saw a human form huddled against the gate of a small garden. Thinking that help was needed, I stretched out my hand. The sobbing increased. From the fair, tousled hair, I gathered that the crouching figure was that of a young woman.

She kept her face buried in her hands, ignoring my offer. Irresolute and weary, I sat down beside her.

The sobbing gradually lessened. I had guessed correctly. It was a girl, young and attractive, as she sat up to thank me, at the same time asking me to go on my way.

The temperature was mild, the full moon shone kindly, so I did not move. Slowly she relaxed, and, after a while told me her story. A story not very different from many others, as I learnt later. She had reached Marseille, having fled with her parents from Strasbourg. The roads were crowded. A low-flying plane had machine-gunned the stream of refugees and her father had been killed before her eyes. She and her mother had succeeded in getting to the Mediterranean, but within a short time her mother had died from exhaustion and grief.

She had more or less managed to survive, rather less than more, taking snapshots of passers-by in the Old Harbour quarter, trying to sell them but with little success.

Running out of money and films, bereft of hope, she had decided to put an end to her life. But at twenty there is a wide gap between decision and act. She had wandered aimlessly through the city, until she had collapsed where I found her.

'My name is Jacqueline. What's yours?'

The ice had broken. We talked until dawn. I offered her a small sum of money to buy films. She accepted, but only as a short-term loan, and we parted as friends and decided to meet again that same evening.

I returned to the station to have a wash in the toilets and, unshaven, carrying my small suitcase, I made my way to the rue de Rome, to a café owned by Albert, a former Marine, warmly recommended to me in London.

The description I had been given fitted the man perfectly.

Broad-shouldered, with a buccaneer's ugly mug and a pipe in his mouth, Albert, serving his customers, looked as I figured he would.

'Youki sent me' I whispered into his ear, acting as I thought a perfect secret agent should, according to Hollywood standards.

Standing behind the counter, seemingly unimpressed, Albert did not bother to answer, carrying on with his work. It was not very encouraging. Making sure no customers could listen, I insisted boldly,

'Youki needs care!'

'What stops you doing what's necessary?' was Albert's joking reply.

Disconcerted, I gave up. I ordered some *Ersatz* coffee and tossed it down. Then before leaving, I leaned towards him and said:

'I'll be back later!'

There was no reaction.

This first setback worried me immensely. Nevertheless, my immediate concern was to find a room. So I started my hunt systematically. Sent from one address to another, I crossed the whole city.

At last I succeeded in renting a room from a woman street-vendor in the rue Longues-des-Capucines, a narrow bustling street mainly lined with foodshops. The spice-vendor's call 'twenty centimes the herb', repeated over and over, has remained engraved in my memory. The room was neat, tiled in red, but the wall of the house in front was at arm's length from my window.

Anyhow, I had a roof over my head!

At noon, I returned to the rue de Rome.

'A coffee, please,' I ordered in a loud voice.

Albert got up very slowly, poured out something called coffee, handed it to me over the counter, and drawing his head closer to mine, peered at me searchingly.

'What's Youki?'

I burnt my boats.

'Youki is Muselier's bitch. He has sent me and told me I could trust you.'

'What for?' asked Albert suspiciously.

'To join the scuffle', I retorted.

He scratched his chin thoughtfully.

I pressed home my advantage.

'Look at my passport: Portuguese visa, Spanish pass. I'm coming from London and can prove it.'

'It is impossible to cross Spain,' objected Albert, and his face hardened.

'Quite true, it is impossible, but I did it.' And I told him about my adventures.

'Come back tomorrow at the same time', he suggested, not quite convinced. 'One of my friends will be here and you'd better take care if you're spinning a yarn. Think it over!'

I nodded.

'I'll be here tomorrow.'

I met Jacqueline in the late afternoon, near the Old Harbour. Together we felt more secure in this overcrowded and overkeyed up city. Without wasting words, I asked her to help me carry out a dangerous task, confessing my ignorance as to how to tackle it.

She accepted before even understanding what it was all about. Eventually she asked me, but I remained evasive.

'I and a group of friends who trust each other, have decided to help those under stress to escape imprisonment and maltreatment.'

44

'You wish to become a good Samaritan?' exclaimed Jacqueline.

I shrugged my shoulders.

'Something of the kind, but whatever is in store, it is an operation that requires loyalty.'

'That suits me fine. It will give a meaning to my existence. What am I supposed to do?'

I knew well that my request would astound her.

'To start with, get some pigeon droppings.'

'Some what?'

'Quite so'. Her bewilderment was amusing.' I need this stuff to write love-letters to Rhea.'

'Who's Rhea?' Jacqueline was irritated.

'Don't be curious. It's much better not to know certain details. Pigeon droppings diluted in water produce an excellent invisible ink. It's not too an attractive liquid — I admit — but spread on paper, for instance, between the lines of a letter, it disappears after drying. By a process known by the addressee, it can be made visible.'

Jacqueline looked sulky.

'I understand and I don't. This is so unexpected. I can't help being curious. But I'll certainly try to avoid asking awkward questions.'

The evening ended gaily and that's how I recruited my first assistant.

The following day, I found Albert sitting at a table in a small room next to the café. By him sat a middle-aged man with a stout face and piercing eyes. Albert brought me a glass of white wine, and then abruptly addressed his friend.

'Here's Henri! It is for you to decide what kind of fellow he is —!'

The other didn't answer but introduced himself.

'My name is Fernand. I know your story. It is rather far-fetched but neither Albert nor I are fools. So if you are working for one of these official or parallel police-services and if you believe that you can incite us to 'spontaneous admissions', so as to foster your promotion, you'd better say so now. Later it might be too late.'

I protested my good faith with the energy of someone who knows that the outcome of the argument would have a decisive effect on the success or failure of his future activity. I needed help and I began to realise how difficult things were going to be. Alone I was doomed. Even those I came to enrol feared falling into the trap of an *agent provocateur* and they would certainly not hesitate to do away with me, if they felt I was one of them.

Therefore, I related one by one the stages of my adventurous passage through Spain. The conversation lasted a long time but I won my point. To my relief, Fernand accepted my story and turning to Albert, agreed that he thought it was genuine.

'Henri tells the truth. Certain details cannot be invented. I think we can help him.'

Albert who had kept silent listening, exclaimed joyfully:

'It's O.K. with me! I am under the Admiral's orders. Let's drink to his health.'

'How does your connection with London work?' asked Fernand, after having emptied his glass. 'It's a crucial matter.'

I had to admit that for the time being it was not quite satisfactory, but that later on steps would be taken to improve it.

'I hope so,' insisted Fernand. 'I'm harbouring a man: Emilio, an Italian friend who has escaped from Mussolini's jails. Ask your Service for permission to send him to England. As a member of the Italian Socialist Party, he will play a major political part. He is a prominent personality.'

I promised to do so without delay, somewhat astonished that my first customer would be a citizen of an enemy country.

I enquired bluntly:

'Is it possible to arrange a departure from Marseille, and, if so, how?'

Fernand smiled.

'Sea communications between Marseille and Beirut, as well as between Marseille and Latin America have been re-established. From Beirut there are merely forty miles to Palestine and the British Forces. The route to South America passes through Gibraltar. The Royal Navy stops and searches all ships crossing the Straits. This could be used to our advantage. I am an active member of the Seamen's Union in this harbour. I have good contacts, and co-operation can be bought. Do you have any funds?'

'It all depends on the amount, but I'll ask right away for more and I will certainly get it.'

'There is something that worries me', I added. 'How do I find candidates wishing to escape, longing to fight? To begin with, they should be of interest to the Allies! I'm thinking in particular of army men and technicians stranded over here.'

'I'll look into that', Fernand promised. 'I can learn from my friends. They know those idling around the harbour, looking for opportunities to leave. I am a Corsican' — his face broadened to a grin — 'Corsican fraternity is a fact. We are used to helping each other. Where do you live?'

I told him.

'To begin with, it might be O.K. But for many reasons it would be better to settle in a place where nobody would think of looking for you. The police are very active, with informers everywhere. It's better to disappear than to appear. Go to Fanny! I'll warn her. She is a Greek brothel-keeper in the Old Harbour district. To her you'll be Mister Henri with ambiguous interests. She rents rooms by the hour. Some of them are unfurnished and therefore available for our future customers. Pay her a fair rent and you will be able to house parcels awaiting shipment. Furthermore, the girls supply excellent intelligence through their clients. It's up to you!'

I agreed. 'I'll settle there as soon as you have talked to her.'

Fernand got up and stretched out his hand.

'Albert knows where to find me. So long!'

8

I do not intend to relate each event in chronological order. My purpose is to underline my evolution, as a result of the exceptional circumstances which I experienced. They transformed the sceptic and rationalist into one who recognised the importance and meaning of life.

If my experience can help the reader to enlarge his vision, then my purpose has been attained.

It seems absurd that only the heavy pressure of circumstances should enable one to overcome the effects arising from inhabiting a mental universe conditioned by family, social and political surroundings, reinforced by upbringing, and education. All these factors to a certain extent imprison each of us and hamper an essential discovery, particularly if they provide an illusion of security to which we cling.

During the war, I discovered a new dimension of our universe. Without prejudice to the sequence of facts, I shall narrate first the relevant events which produced a fundamental change, leading from a formerly austere and rigid outlook to open mindedness, and an optimistic approach to difficulties encountered, thanks to understanding and accepting an exploration necessary to clear the way to happiness.

The months I spent in Marseille influenced me strongly. Much later I understood that epoch through the assertion of a Zen master, whom I met after the war in the Black Forest. He was teaching archery to youngsters, and I learned from him that Heaven can only be attained through our exploration of our subconscious inferno.

I explored my inferno during the most difficult period of my existence; it was indeed a dark period, illuminated by some clear, faint rays.

Jacqueline's unfaltering friendship was one of them.

It is not easy after so long a time to give a picture of a woman seen through the clouded rear mirror of stress and strain caused by the clandestine operations we were committed to.

Frail, blonde Jacqueline accepted danger with voluptuous pleasure; its subtle poison wiped out the emptiness left by her parents' death.

She continued her roving photographer's job in the Old Harbour, an activity not without risk of unpleasant solicitations.

Her loyalty was touching. In spite of our ever closer relationship, she never uttered a word of reproach about the behaviour of Mr. Henri, an individual with unspecified business interests, recommended by Fernand to Fanny the Greek.

I had, in fact, rented one of the upper rooms in the latter's disreputable hotel, more brothel than hotel, a place of anonymous comings and goings.

Faithful to the identity I had assumed, I managed to remain on friendly terms with the boarders, without — for obvious reasons — accepting any intimacy. But I took care not to offend those who offered me their charms free of charge.

In contrast to the foul slums of the Old Harbour, Paul's apartment became a heavenly shelter.

I had met Paul — a member of one of the oldest Marseille families — by chance in Albert's café. We immediately clicked and he invited me to his home.

I found there the human warmth I so greatly needed. His advice and help were always available and he welcomed me, a stranger, into his family, where I enjoyed the serene atmosphere born of mutual trust.

The Mers-el-Kebir attack had deeply upset Paul. Although approving General de Gaulle's appeal, his patriotism could never accept the idea of Frenchmen fighting Frenchmen. This attitude did not prevent me from confiding my mission, as well as my worries, and in spite of the risks his family would have to face in the event of my arrest, he encouraged me to visit him as often as I liked.

It was in Jacqueline's tiny room that I wrote my passionate

love-letters to Rhea; thanks to the pigeon droppings she collected from an ample supply in church squares, I was able to inform the Service of my set-up, financial needs, and first results.

Equally passionate answers came in reply and the censors, who had to examine our mail, must have had quite a time reading our lyrical outpourings.

Between the lines in the exact sense of the words, I was told that a messenger would deliver the requested funds and that Emilio, the Italian, was permitted to enter Great Britain. Much good advice followed. They concerned mostly security requirements, urging me, in the immediate future, not to get in touch with different Resistance groups considered unsafe at the present stage. I should stick to my objective, prepare exfiltration possibilities but avoid compromising contacts in the interest of speed. The escape network should be ready to operate at full efficiency later, particularly for airmen forced to bale out over France.

My relationship with Fernand was cordial, and we decided that the first escape voyage would be organised in the middle of September. Two sailors of the *Mariette Pacha*, a steamer on the Beirut line, had agreed, against payment, to prepare a hiding-place in the hold, and to facilitate the embarkation of the parcels, promising to supply them with food during the trip.

Fernand had informed me that in the city a Polish pilot was sheltered by another Pole whom he knew. I went to see him and found a worried man, dreading gossiping neighbours. He was most relieved by my offer to take his friend away and lodge him in Fanny's place.

On another day, strolling along the Old Harbour docks, Jacqueline and I noticed a crowd gathered round a man lying in the gutter.

'It's a foolish Englishman', said a woman, standing at her shell-fish stall.

'He won't get up, maybe he is sick. We ought to call the police.'

I lost no time, and bending over the man lying on his

belly, his head resting on his arms, I whispered in his native tongue,

'Are you English?'

'Go to hell', he said. 'I'm fed up. Get it over with and have me arrested.'

'Can you get up?', I seized his arm, while Jacqueline tried loudly to convince the onlookers that fortunately no Englishman could possibly be in Marseille.

'I can, but I won't', he retorted.

'You damned fool', I said, 'get up and follow me, I'll help you.'

He raised his head, stared at me incredulously and jumped to his feet.

I was already leading the way, while Jacqueline went on talking volubly.

Walking fast, I hurried him along, turning my head occasionally in case we were being followed, and eventually reached Fanny's place safely.

Settled on a mattress spread on the floor of one of the attic rooms, I questioned the stranger sitting cross-legged in front of me.

'I escaped', he explained, 'from a prison camp near Dunkirk. I'm a major in an infantry regiment. We had to surrender because we were encircled. Some civilians helped me with clothing and food. We tramped from one farm to another, sometimes getting a lift from supply-trucks. I'm glad to say I didn't have to conceal my nationality. Not all Frenchmen are anti-English.'

'They aren't,' I agreed, 'at least not yet. But you were bloody lucky not to be denounced.'

'Maybe', acknowledged my newly-acquired parcel. 'I arrived in Marseille, not knowing where the hell to go, what to do, or whom to see. I went to the American Consulate, but they showed me the door, pretending to be neutral. Our brothers across the Atlantic did not act very brotherly.'

'Yes', I said.

'So, what to do? I wandered through this wretched city for

two days without food or sleep and then I collapsed. You know the rest.'

'You were in danger of arrest', I reminded him.

He shrugged his shoulders. 'So what? Everything has an end.'

'Sometimes, one just feels like 'Damn it all', and if I express myself so mildly, it is because in my family bad words are taboo.'

His complexion had taken a turn for the better. My unexpected help was cheering him up. He went on:

'All over France the urge for freedom kept me going. But here in Marseille there was the sea. Suddenly, I saw thousands of people apparently unconcerned with the war; in fact, I found a world I didn't understand.'

He sighed deeply, his eyes gazing at me searchingly as if to read my inner thoughts. Suddenly, he burst out:

'Are you Jesus Christ or what? I thought I didn't believe any longer in Santa Claus.'

I laughed. 'Nevertheless, he exists, and now you have the proof of it! Listen! There are two fellow travellers between these walls. It is against the rules to go downstairs, sleep with the girls, or make a noise. Those who saw you come in will think you may have left. There's a lot of ins and outs going on in this house. So you must give your word, and I'll do my best to get you out. Now, I'll try to rustle up some food.'

A Belgian, a specialist in electronics — a new and promising science — soon completed the foursome ready for departure. Fernand had learned through a Corsican friend that the Belgian had approached a fisherman. Jacqueline found the Belgian and brought him to me.

Everything was set, but the sinews of war were cruelly missing. My courier failed to show up. His unexplained delay could have dramatic consequences. I had no money to pay Fanny, who was beginning to look at me doubtfully. Fernand could not understand the reason for the delay and rejected my explanations.

The reputation of the English Secret Services was at stake.

The patience of my 'Musketeers', as I called them, consigned to the attic, was wearing thin. Only later, I learnt that they plotted behind my back, either through fear of having fallen into a trap or simply because claustrophobia was making them jittery, to escape from a place they regarded as a prison.

Albert, whom I visited every morning for a cup of real chocolate, warned me about the psychological effects of the situation.

Jacqueline, gentle and well-balanced by nature was also growing anxious, although she did not say so. As for me, I had no other recourse than to write more love-letters to Rhea, which had lately remained unanswered.

Subsequently, I learnt the cause. The Service had delegated a clerk from the Madrid Embassy to hand over a suitcase with a false bottom containing money to a Spanish courier who had agreed to bring it to me in Marseille. The clerk had been caught while peacefully lunching in an inn situated in the prohibited area near the Pyrenees. He was to meet the courier near by. The Spanish policemen discovered the false bottom, kept the cash, and jailed the clerk. He was only released after repeated representations through diplomatic channels, which lasted several weeks.

The affair had repercussions in London. The Service, called to order by the official diplomatic authorities, had to find other ways of communication, and this took time. They lacked information on what the arrested clerk might have revealed, and especially the courier. The latter, who had disappeared, knew my address, so the Service preferred not to answer my appeals for help, at least temporarily.

My position in Marseille became almost impossible. Ignored by London, regarded with suspicion by my friends, cut off from my family — for security reasons I had told nobody of my return to France — I brooded gloomily, almost near despair.

To understand the picture properly, one must imagine Mr. Henri, a man with no ties, living in a brothel in a city seething with contradictory rumours, surrounded by prostitutes night and day, trying to keep his head on his shoulders. The girls were actually decent, moreso than one might imagine. They were vulgar, describing their sexual exploits, readily revealing their flabby bodies, miming obscene gestures to illustrate the vices enjoyed by their customers, but friendly to the lonely man I seemed to be.

One should also understand that Mr. Henri was supposed to have a 'bizness', however undefined, and that he was expected to find his surroundings quite normal. Furthermore, Fanny who was much smarter than she looked, half-suspected that Mr. Henri was organising clandestine departures. One day, she even attempted to cash in on her suspicions by asking him to blackmail, in her stead, a former boarder who had married a well-to-do man totally ignorant of her past.

'You're an educated man! Go to Jocelyne, show her these letters. They're worth a lot of gold. Whatever the price she offers, we'll share.'

Mr. Henri expressed his incompetence in such matters and politely declined, but he felt the threat.

Yes! I was touching the depths. The date fixed for the parcels shipment was approaching and Rhea had still shown no sign of life. One morning, shaving in front of the kitchen sink which served as a wash-room, the cracked steamy mirror reflected the image of a broken man.

'Who are you?' I asked my reflection. 'Just a nobody, a shadowy figure. A shadow invented by anonymous individuals in an organisation which has now written you off. Poor fool! You were in search of heroism and adventure. Well, you got all you wanted and more. You're wearing a false beard in a brothel. You're quite alone, left to your own devices. Your family believes you're dead on the field of honour. What a splendid joke! You'll die like a rat among the other rats of this city, where everybody and everything stinks. These poor chaps upstairs believe you are Jesus Christ. You are Don Quixote in his undershorts, a doleful knight, that's what you are. Do they even know that the silence on the other side of the Channel will shortly deliver you and those who trust you to the gallows. And if they do, they couldn't care less!'

54

While muttering these phrases, maybe to give myself courage, I perceived Garcia's face in the mirror, like a mirage projected by my tortured mind.

My heart began to beat rapidly. I remembered his words:

'Don't forget my advice.'

I *had* quite forgotten it, and the time had come to make good my omission. Instantly I returned to my room.

'The magic power of silence must be tested, now or never', I told myself.

I lay down and tried to forget myself and my fears.

'The conscious self must be an unbiased witness', Garcia had said.

'To perceive the message, the unbiased witness must be totally unaffected by the object's considerations.'

I was the object, the unbiased witness was my higher self. Looking at myself, so to speak, from above. I was floating between the ceiling and the floor, with a strange sensation of being under water. I saw myself lying on the bed, understanding that the one who was observing the outstretched form was not my physical self but my higher one, immersed in deep silence, as if detached from my physical reality.

I realise that it is difficult, if not impossible, to recall a mood, almost a dissociation, leading to another dimension. The body, the earth, the stars, one's self are floating in a chamber of eternity. Physical reality dissolves. Overwhelming problems appear negligible. Relinquishment of the normal mechanism of thought brings about an impulse comparable to a throbbing prayer, while return is experienced as an immense calmness.

One feels identified with the universe, with the eternal and the infinite. Marseille and Fanny's brothel disintegrated into nothingness.

My brain seemed numb, but I could perceive things differently now. Thanks to an unknown faculty, the obvious, until then hidden, emerged as an instant of truth, illuminating my entire being; an immense clarity invaded my inner self.

Garcia's words re-echoed in my subconscious mind but no subjective thought interfered with the echo.

'Open the door of the secret place of your soul to reach comprehension. Be the mediator between your inner reality and the hostile world confronting you. You cannot solve your difficulties by using false arguments, but only by understanding your inner self and knowing the right action to take. Be silent mentally, inwardly, and the rest will be granted you.'

He was right.

It was in this silence that suddenly flashed the solution to the problem which had lately completely absorbed me.

I saw it so clearly that I did not doubt the outcome. The spell was broken and I returned to my normal state. I sprang up, dressed quickly and rushed out in search of Jacqueline to inform her of my decision to leave with her for Monaco the same evening.

'Well, well!' said Jacqueline, flabbergasted by my cheerfulness, 'you've certainly changed since yesterday.'

A deep unknown joy had taken the place of my previous anxiety. My present peace of mind was driving me to action, to an apparently foolish action whose success I never doubted. Thanks to the serenity born from total detachment — a word which can be understood only by those who have experienced it — I felt newly born.

9

It is a long way from theory to practice. I cannot pretend to have achieved immediately the escape described by mystics, an escape beyond the boundaries of a mental universe burdened with problems.

Undoubtedly, the strain due to a situation apparently without issue had helped me to pass beyond whatever oppressed me, and so I experienced for the first time the beneficent feeling born by acceptance of the unacceptable. It might be translated by 'So be it', a state of mind which is indeed an act of faith.

To pass beyond, to accept the unacceptable, induces an intuitive comprehension on a level of awareness unaffected by fear, whatever form it may take. I saw the causes of human conflict, of wars waged because men are unaware of the truth. I saw the uselessness of both victories and defeats. I saw that the true theatre of war is not where the battle is waged, nor where the canons are thundering. It is where minds are perverted by systems and doctrines, where freedom is lost, freedom of choice alone corresponds to the yearning of the inner being. I saw the folly of transitory victories which are but ephemeral truces never leading to the supreme peace I had experienced in that uplifting moment.

In this state beyond, I visualised a possible solution to my immediate problems, based on an apparently absurd belief. I was convinced, nevertheless, that it would be successful. This total confidence cannot be explained. It springs from the depths of one's self and has no rational basis.

I was perfectly aware of the hazards of gambling. I knew how small the chances are of winning at the tables. But I never doubted the necessity for my venture. Even the wish to win was absent. I knew that Monte Carlo was the only casino that had not closed its doors, and I knew that I had to go there in order to carry out a mission entrusted to me. I had no money, but in my state of euphoria I never doubted that it would materialise.

Each noon, Fanny shared her meal with her boarders, since the girls began their work only in the early afternoon. She presided at the head of the table, proud to be the mistress, and at such times was in an amenable mood. I entered the room at the end of the meal. Fanny, picking her teeth with a knitting-needle, looked up enquiringly. I beckoned to her. She rose, and in a far corner, I requested bluntly:

'A loan of thirty thousand francs, Fanny. For forty-eight hours. Just to take delivery of a consignment of goods. A perfectly sound deal which will bring me fifty thousand francs in cash. We'll share the profit.'

Her eyes sparkled.

'Do you mean you'll give me back my cash plus twentyfive grand?'

'Yes', I confirmed. 'My friends upstairs are your security. Besides, you know I'm not the man to play dirty.'

'It's a deal', she agreed. 'But don't you dare make me regret it.'

'I won't. Quite the contrary.'

At six p.m. that day Jacqueline and I reached the Saint Charles railway station. In my memory, the compartment we found, the gloomy, darkened light, the crammed corridor, and the man and the woman sitting by the window intermingle and overlap. I recognised the couple immediately, but I was Henri Jonquière and he was not acquainted with them.

The young woman kept staring at me. My moustache only slightly changed my looks.

'It's he,' she exclaimed. 'It's Frédéric! Why does he pretend not to recognise us?'

She called out over the other passengers' heads:

'Frédéric, don't make a fool of yourself. Say hello to us!'

I sat silently trying to look unconcerned. The man hesitated.

'There is a likeness', he decided, 'but it is not Frédéric.'

Everybody in the compartment was staring at me. It was a dangerous situation. Any of the passengers might turn out to be a policeman, or a citizen hungry for self importance ready to turn informer. The young woman's insistence was frightening. Jacqueline, white as a sheet, immediately understood. She was suddenly aware that Henri Jonquière was not my real name and rightly feared that, in case of a serious check I would be unmasked.

An uneasy silence. The bluish light bulb, casting a dim light, added to the unreality.

My heart was hammering. To overcome the feeling of helplessness I counted its beats while the young woman kept looking at me.

She was convinced she was right. She was sure of it, and offended not to be believed. So she kept repeating.

'It is he, I tell you it is he!'

My heart went on hammering. The minutes dragged on. Jacqueline and I were on tenterhooks and each jolt of the train increased our fears.

Finally we reached Nice without further adventures, and how great was our relief. Cautiously we withdrew to a waiting-room to let the flow of passengers pass through the station. At last, after quite a time, we left and found an hotel for the night since no train was leaving for Monte Carlo until the morning.

The principality of Monaco seemed like another world. The blackout was less strict and the atmosphere everywhere more relaxed.

Monte Carlo looked to us like a musical comedy setting. The old fashioned stucco structure of the Casino, the palm trees and blooming shrubs, the people sipping aperitifs and gossiping conveyed the impression of submerged universe. We entered the Casino. Our footsteps rang on the marble floor.

'Have you been here before?' asked the inspector to whom we applied for entry cards.

'No' I lied, hoping that Henri Jonquière — the real one — had had no such opportunity.

He consulted his card index, satisfying himself that such was the case, and after checking our identity papers filled in our cards.

'Thank goodness!' sighed Jacqueline.

'Frédéric, what good wind brings you here?'

As if stung by a scorpion I swung round, drops of sweat on my forehead. A former friend.

'I'm afraid I don't know you', I answered, my voice shaking.

Grasping the entry cards the Inspector was still holding, I moved away as quickly as possible. Trying to look unconcerned, I said to Jacqueline, 'Come, let's go to the gaming rooms'. She followed, shaken but courageous.

An usher showed me to an empty seat at a *chemin de fer* table. I sat down, apprehensively, expecting to see the inspector appear. I knew how tough the supervision was.

Fortunately, nothing happened.

'The bank is yours', announced the croupier, sliding the dealing box forward.

Twenty-five thousand francs in the bank! I pushed the chips towards the middle of the table and dealt the cards.

Jacqueline told me the subsequent events, because my brain was not working normally. At the first deal, I turned up a nine. Banco had been requested.

'Followed', announced the person who had lost.

I dealt anew.

'No cards', he declared after looking at the two in his hand.

I turned mine, one knave and a four and took one more - a five.

'Nine to the bank', announced the croupier.

'Followed', repeated the loser.

I dealt out the cards. My opponent barely glanced at them and announced:

'Eight!'

'Nine to the bank', said the croupier impassively, as I turned up the King of Spades and the nine of Hearts.

I listened to my voice, declaring.

'The bank passes.'

Throughout the game, I had acted as an automaton. At no time had I taken part in what was going on. I remained unconcerned. Gathering up the chips, representing about one hundred and fifty thousand francs, I got up after distributing tips, hurried to the pay-desk, and from there to the exit, Jacqueline at my heels. My only thought was to leave Monte Carlo immediately.

We reached the station, a train was steaming in; we climbed into a coach and left the Principality. I found a seat, closed my eyes and do not remember feeling any satisfaction. Exhausted, as if emptied of everything, I fell asleep.

No conclusion should be drawn from this game of cards. The Goddess of Chance, the sceptics may say, managed things well. I know today that chance is but the visible manifestation of an intricate number of circumstances, whose interactions result in what we call chance. But why speculate.

This good fortune restored my reputation with those who had mistrusted me. Thanks to the money so strangely acquired, the first departure to the free world took place, but only at the second attempt, since the first one ended almost in disaster.

The long expected evening had arrived at last. Around midnight, I escorted our four parcels to a small, usually padlocked, gate in the railings surrounding the harbour wharves. Marius, one of the two sailors who had promised their help, opened it stealthily to take them over. They were more moved than they wished to admit. I shook hands. They whispered their thanks and left. And that I thought was that. But man proposes and God disposes.

That same evening we saw them again; and, needless to say, it was not a happy reunion.

Marius knew that he could — in an emergency — find me at Albert's café. I had told him I would spend the night there.

A knock before daybreak at the door of the café made us fear the worst. It was Marius and our friends, but to know that they were safe made us sigh with relief. Marius did not bother to explain. He disappeared at once, hastening back to his ship. It was the Belgian who told the story of their adventure.

To spare the stowaways an extremely uncomfortable first night, Marius had hidden them in his own cabin which he shared with the ship's baker. Knowing that the latter never

61

embarked until the very last minute because of his wife and children, he decided to keep them there until dawn. But the exception confirms the rule. That night, a family quarrel drove the baker out of his home. Having tried to drown his sorrows in alcohol, he reached the ship dead drunk. Finding his cabin locked, he shouted furiously and drummed on the door, not understanding why he couldn't get in.

Fortunately, the Duty officer took no notice of his curses, and Marius was able to calm him down. Nevertheless, he thought it prudent to disembark everybody, and to take the parcels back to Albert's café.

It was certainly a setback, but the whole affair could have ended in disaster. Fernand, whom we phoned to meet us, was seriously upset.

'This hullabaloo may lead to trouble', was his comment. 'We must carry out another operation at the earliest possible moment. I'll see to it.'

He did. Within two days the necessary was done and the clandestine embarkation repeated. This time on a boat bound for Latin America.

'Write to your English friends to strengthen their control in Gibraltar', recommended Fernand. 'But even if your letter arrives too late, the ship will be searched from top to bottom before proceeding through the Straits. Our parcels are bound to be discovered.'

I was convinced and confident. The journey to Gibraltar was shorter than to Beirut, and our venture was totally successful.

To travel in a concealed nook at the bottom of the hold is not particularly pleasant. Darkness and sea-sickness are serious impediments. Fernand, more aware than I of the kind of danger this sort of operation conceals, insisted on making the Service understand that in future it should take its responsibilities and make the necessary arrangements to enable us to continue our efforts. Deserted creeks earmarked for such operations would allow discreet embarkation on small vessels which could approach undetected.

'Go to Sete. My friend Secco, the local secretary of the

Seamen's Trade Union, is hiding an important man. We call him 'General' although he does not bear a military rank. He is Secretary General of a trade union, and he should leave for Gibraltar quickly, as he is liable to arrest. Secco can no longer shelter him. In view of his reputation, he will be welcomed with open arms by the Free French. It's your job to notify them. We'll wait for help from London. We have proved that we are reliable; now it's up to London to provide the means to carry on.'

I agreed entirely. To repeat the Monte Carlo exploit was unthinkable, and the chances of a return to Paris took shape in my mind.

'I'll invent a likely tale to explain my long absence,' I told myself. 'I'll see my parents again. Once back home, I could without saying too much make them understand what I was involved in.'

I informed Jacqueline of my plan; she was ready to accompany me, wanting to use this opportunity to get to Alsace and find out if the property abandoned at the time of her flight was still there.

However, I decided to wait another month, so as not to miss the arrival of a messenger with instructions from London.

In any case London would know how to find me. I could also — in the Occupied Zone — try to establish useful contacts and a few safe-houses where parcels could hide awaiting transport opportunities, once the connection with the Service had been resumed.

Consequently, I wrote a long love letter to Rhea and left for Sete.

Secco greeted me with obvious pleasure.

'I've heard about you', he said. 'And I've got my little plan. I know how to get the General away. The Royal Navy must send a small craft from Gibraltar to meet him. It's up to you to take every precaution to ensure his safe arrival.'

'Who is the General, and when am I going to see him?'

'You'll soon meet him. He shaved his beard off so as not to be recognised. You'll have to imagine it as you may have seen his photograph in the past.'

Secco talked rapidly, his eyes shining. Bubbling with vitality, he hurried me off to meet two friends of his; Daddy Lenk, as he called him, and his son.

'They have a good seagoing craft, half-fishing half-pleasure boat. Lenk Junior knows how to sail it. They are Alsatians, and Jacques, the son, wants to join De Gaulle. A fishing-boat can slip out of port at the right moment. As for supplies and fuel, something might be arranged. I know where to get it. Transport won't be easy but we'll find a way. *La Mangouste,* Lenk Senior's boat, is anchored not far from the pier, and easy to get at.'

My mind was elsewhere. Here I was back in Sete. The memory of my not-so-distant previous passage caused my thoughts to travel towards two little girls. I remembered them resting on the luggage trolleys at the station. What were they doing now? Had the bombs which — according to German communiques — had flattened England, spared them?

We slowly climbed the shady path, leading to the top of one of the hills surrounding the city. Stopping to admire the view, I realised dumbfounded that a vessel anchored in port was the *Aurora.*

'What ship is that?' I asked, pointing towards it.

'It's an old tub belonging to two brothers', replied Secco. 'They left Sete at the time of the Armistice with twenty Belgian diamond merchants and a few others on board. The *Aurora,* that's her name, sails under Panamanian colours, but the brothers are Greek. Did they land the merchants on a deserted beach of the Palestine coast, or did they drown them to keep their diamonds, that's the question? All I can say is that they have some bloody cheek to show their faces here again. If they dared to come back, they must certainly be able to leave again. I really don't know how, unless they bribed some high-ups.'

Strange, very strange, I thought. For the third time I was brought face to face with this ship, as if fate had placed it purposely in my way.

However, I made no comment.

'We're arriving' — announced Secco pushing open a gate in

the railings surrounding a well-kept garden. The Lenks welcomed us cordially. We discussed the subject at once. I quickly saw that Secco had prepared the ground as the father raised no objection to his plan.

'If Jacques considers it's his duty to enlist in the Free French Forces', he said, 'he should do so. France is on her knees but maybe she is willing to rise again. Although....' He did not finish the sentence.

Jacques agreed enthusiastically.

'With one thousand litres of fuel, we can evade any police pursuit and not depend solely on the wind. I'm sure we'll succeed. The question is, how can we obtain the fuel?'

Secco rubbed his chin.

'Everything can be bought if you knock at the right door. I believe I know the door.'

He did. The next evening, around midnight, Jacques and I were rowing, seated in a dinghy, towards the cache hiding six barrels of fuel oil camouflaged behind a heap of scrap iron. Three trips would be required, we thought, to remove them in the manner Secco had suggested.

'Oil being lighter than water, the barrels will float,' he said. 'A rowing boat on the channel crossing the town is not noticeable at night. To tow the barrels behind the boat is just a pleasure trip! And we'll be waiting for you on *La Mangouste*.'

The first trip went off smoothly. This success encouraged us. The second was different. We may have relaxed our attention on our way back. Suddenly, rather late, we caught sight of a drunkard staggering along the channel, talking loudly to himself. We did not stop, since we expected him to move away. This was a mistake! Seeing us, he started to abuse us, accompanying our dinghy along the quay and continuing his insults. How to get rid of him? Jacques was rowing with all his strength, the boat was skimming along fast, but the drunkard kept pace. Casting caution to the winds, Jacques rowed even more frantically, but the towed oil drums hampered our advance. Irritated by the fool's yelling, I had difficulty in keeping them under control. The drums started knocking against each other, scraping the canal walls.

The noise they made was terrific! Shutters opened, curses were hurled, minutes passed, each one an eternity.

I could hear Jacques panting. At last, his efforts were rewarded. The noise lessened, then stopped. We had entered the dock area. Exhausted, we waited a long time before nearing *La Mangouste*.

When we reached her, dawn was breaking. Daddy Lenk and Secco had waited anxiously. With superhuman efforts we hoisted our cargo on board.

We had been blessed with the most incredible luck. Crossing the city from one end to another in such dangerous conditions and avoiding arrest seemed almost impossible!

Impossible is not French! And so we undertook the third and last trip which had a different kind of surprise in store. We were half-way along the channel, when we heard the sound of a marching troop.

One, two, one, two...

A dog barked above our heads, the boat scraped against the rough walls of the channel. Jacques stiffened on the thwart and drew in the oars.

Crouched behind, holding the rope and tying the oil drums with one hand, I was desperately trying to prevent them from colliding.

The channel was narrow, its walls not very high, and the men whom we guessed to be near, would doubtless sooner or later cast a glance on the motionless water. They would see us and the game would be up.

The footsteps were drawing nearer and nearer. We instinctively closed our eyes. At any moment the challenge would come.

It was three a.m. The moonless night was dark, but the stars were shining too brightly for our peace of mind.

'Halt', ordered a voice.

The sound of footsteps ceased — my heart stopped beating.

'Disperse', said the voice in a martial tone.

Up there, almost within arm's reach, the men didn't wait

for the order to be repeated. We heard doors bang.

Silence fell suddenly. Incredible but true. Then in the silence a dog started barking. He had spotted us. He continued barking. Somewhere a shutter creaked, the thud of an object crashing on a soft surface made the animal howl and run off yelping. An irate citizen had rescued us from a new danger suspended — in the truest sense of the word — over our heads.

Jacques had already grasped the oars; he gently dipped them into the water and our noiseless re-advance started. I tried to control the drums, bought at an enormous price from a city scrap merchant, the price of freedom for the General. I had not yet met him, but I had guessed his identity.

We soon entered the deep waters of the dock and moored our dinghy alongside *La Mangouste*.

Four hands stretched out. Without a word, straining and pulling, we hoisted the two last barrels onto the gangway.

'That's it', said Jacques, looking at his father, who was filling his pipe.

Secco was rubbing his hands. Corsican to the core, anything to do with smuggling delighted him on principle.

The four of us returned to the jetty.

Secco disappeared to the right, while I followed Daddy Lenk and son to their house perched high up near the cemetery.

The day set for the departure was now imminent.

'Let us go and see the General', suggested Secco. 'He's the boss. He is in hiding and the risks are very great. Sooner or later, Vichy will try to arrest him. The hunt against the enemies of the present régime is starting. We may as well not deceive ourselves, we'll all soon be called to account and, as Secretary General of a powerful organisation, he more than anyone else.'

I could only agree.

The famous man's cheeks seemed flabbier and his eyelids heavier than in the pictures I had seen. After introducing me, Secco briefly stated the purpose of our visit and the plan for his departure.

'Henri', he asserted boldly, 'has arranged for a Royal Navy

destroyer to meet you halfway. In a few days you'll speak on the B.B.C. Your message will raise hopes.'

'Do our preparations suit you?' I asked the Secretary General.

'Perfectly', he replied. 'I am more than ready. The Free French need a man of my status. Hundreds of thousands of workers are waiting to listen to my voice. My arrival in London will mean a turning point in history.'

I thanked him and assured him that, so far as I was concerned, I had done everything to ensure him a warm welcome. This was true, as I had, right after my interview with Daddy Lenk, written a love-letter, transmitting the necessary information, specifying the parcel's identity and suggesting the despatch of a destroyer to meet him.

The Secretary General shook both my hands effusively.

'I'll never forget what you are doing for me and the Trade Union cause. Thank you. Now I must go and tell Moustique the good news.'

'Moustique?' I asked, once he had left the room.

Secco raised his arms upwards.

'His sweetheart. He is taking her with him. I didn't dare tell you!'

'My God! What will London think?'

Secco shrugged his shoulders unperturbed.

'We shall see!'

Half an hour elapsed. Neither of us could understand the reason for the long delay. Finally the door opened and the Secretary General appeared. Looking grim, he hesitated a few seconds, and then with downcast eyes announced:

'Moustique dreads sea-sickness!'

Seeing my bewilderment, he went on:

'It's a detail to which I attach no importance. None at all. But I have finally decided to stay in France. My conviction tells me to carry on the struggle here. I am not leaving.'

I couldn't believe my ears! So big an effort wasted just because his girl-friend was afraid of being sea-sick.

Secco, dumbfounded, tried to convince him.

'Take advantage of this opportunity, Boss. It's Heaven-sent. You know as well as I do that we are prisoners on bail. Think of the comrades whom your broadcasts would stir to new hope. Think of the papers hidden under my crippled mother's skirts where nobody would dare search for them, so as to enable you to organise effective action in London. For God's sake change your mind!'

His pleadings were to no avail.

'No, I am not leaving without Moustique. That's final!'

I saw that all our arguments were useless. I could only accept the fact and regret it.

We left. Secco, deeply shaken, burst into a fit of nervous laughter.

'What a helluva joke', he repeated several times. 'Fancy listening to such nonsense! What a bloody mess!'

Jacques Lenk was terribly disappointed when I told him the bad news. I promised however to organise his departure at the earliest possible moment. He refused to wait indefinitely and embarked with some friends a month later.

No destroyer came to meet them. An early autumn storm compelled them to take refuge in a Spanish port. Finally, they were captured, and interned for many months, eventually reaching North Africa.

I said good-bye to Secco and left for Marseille, more determined than ever to reach Paris. Jacqueline and I would attempt to cross the demarcation line at a favourable spot, and no doubt Fernand or Albert would be able to tell us where and how.

Inwardly, I exulted. For me, Paris was home!

10

It was raining that autumn day of 1940. A steady downpour, 'a soaker' — was the bar-keeper's comment in Saint-Florent-sur-Cher. Albert had told us to see him on his behalf.

We explained frankly what we wanted and he readily agreed to lead us to a place not far away where it would be possible to crawl under the barbed wire entanglements dividing the so-called Free Zone from the Occupied.

'They haven't yet properly consolidated the frontier', he said. 'A slight slope makes it easy to pass underneath. The guards don't usually have dogs, but I'm afraid things may change soon.'

'Take a rest in a corner of the bar', he added. 'We'll be leaving at five in the morning.'

A cold rain was still falling. The night was dark, the ground slippery. The innkeeper led us to an abandoned quarry and warned us in a low voice.

'Crouch behind these stone blocks. Wait for dawn. The barbed wire is a few yards ahead, a little below our level. A patrol passes every morning. Watch out for it and take your chance a few minutes after it has passed. The Jerries won't be able to see you as the path skirts round the quarry. You have nothing to fear. Once on the other side, dash to a small wood on your left. The road to Bourges is on the other side. You'll get there in time to catch the train to Paris.'

He was right. We saw the patrol coming but, before it passed, we caught a glimpse of a dismal procession: prisoners guarded by a few armed soldiers, dragging their feet, conveying the image of cattle being led to slaughter.

Such was our first brutal contact with the world of constraint. The flapping of the poor fellows' soles, sucked in by the soggy ground, rang in my ears for a long time afterwards.

We hurried to the barbed wire entanglement. I raised some wires with a stick:

'Quickly! Jacqueline, go!'

70

She slipped underneath, and I followed.

We ran to the wood, found the road to Bourges, and took the train to Paris.

Paris, wet under the rain already mixed with melted snow, had an unreal aspect in the bleak wintry light. Yet my pulse quickened as we crossed the river. The good old Seine had not moved from its bed, and the muddy waters flowed placidly on.

Leaning against the parapet, Wehrmacht soldiers were behaving like tourists, watching the changing facets of the water.

We took the subway. Voluptuously, I sniffed the polluted air, its warm and acrid smell, the same as of old. But the old, light-hearted advertisements had gone from the walls. I noticed the placards uniformly extolled the New Order.

The atmosphere too had changed. A perceptible uneasiness seemed to oppress the passengers. 'Each man for himself and God for all' could be read on their faces. It was not until much later that I understood the subtleties and contradictions of the citizens' often paradoxical behaviour. In a sense they had no option but to behave like the ostrich, closing their eyes to what lay ahead. The maxim: 'Sufficient unto the day...' turned into a rule, survival the only concern.

A disparaging press offered scapegoats to an embittered public opinion. Justification of the Armistice, the Black Market and collaboration was the theme of the flood of decrees and proclamations issued by the Vichy government, the German 'Kommandatur' and the various police organisations each zealously competing to threaten or encourage informers, always to be found in such dangerous times.

Even the meaning of words had changed. A kind of tacit complicity enforced new concepts adjusted to the circumstances. The reaction to the shock of the French army's collapse was to glorify the strength of the victor, whose triumph was envied.

Every day German military parades headed for the Champs-Elysées; these parades were nicknamed the 'Circus'. Although people tried to ignore them, the rhythmical march of hand-picked men aroused a subconscious respect.

From the very first day in Paris I was swept into the maelstrom of events, any of which could have annihilated my own plans. Within a few hours I was to learn that it is easier to disappear than to reappear. But it was too late to withdraw.

With a slight jolt the train stopped at the République station. This was where Jacqueline and I had to part. Each of us dreaded the moment of separation. Jacqueline intended to reach Belfort where a relative of hers lived, before making future plans. To penetrate into annexed Alsace required formalities. Once there, she ran the risk of being cut off from Paris for good. Even if she dared not to think about it her eyes revealed her fears.

I could feel her eyes on me as, controlling my own emotions, I strode ahead towards the exit. We said goodbye under the precarious shelter of the oilcloth roof of a derelict newspaper stand.

Jacqueline threw herself into my arms, promising to write Poste Restante. Unaware of what I would find on my return I had thought it preferable not to reveal my true identity or my address. I urged her to join me as soon as possible. She promised she would. Waving farewell, she stood motionless under the oilcloth. Deeply moved, I rushed down the subway steps. I never heard of her again.

A new chapter began as I alighted at the Porte de Champerret station and slowly walked to my home on the Boulevard Victor Hugo in Neuilly.

I believe my hand was shaking when I pressed the bell. I told the *concierge* that I had given no sign of life until now because I had suffered amnesia caused by a shell-burst. The blast, I explained, had not wounded me, but certain brain cells had been affected. Nursed in Bordeaux, I had forgotten everything, including my address.

One should bear in mind that in those days the most unlikely stories would be accepted as normal.

Zell opened the door of my appartment. She started

screaming when she saw me, and was so excited that I had great difficulty in calming her.

'And Madame, and the children?' she asked.

I repeated the tale I had told the *concierge*, pretending that I had experienced the first symptoms of amnesia shortly after our departure from Biarritz.

'Madame has taken the children to an unknown place', I added. 'But I'll do my utmost to find them.'

I am sure she did not believe me, but she accepted my story.

And then Zell told me that my parents had left Paris. They had felt abandoned and extremely worried about their son's fate, and so had made use of their connections to obtain the necessary permits to travel to the Argentine to their married daughter, who lived in Buenos Aires. Their old age had helped to overcome many obstacles, and they had sailed from Marseille only a short time before.

Our ways had probably crossed, unaware that we had been so near each other.

After getting over my first acute disappointment, I realised that freedom from family ties gave me a considerable advantage. Sooner or later, my clandestine activities would have compromised them. It was much better to face the future alone.

I went to the factory I had left only a few months before. My sudden appearance caused a stir. It certainly came as a shock to the manager, André Buchois. He had taken over my job convinced that I would not return. He had sold everything of market value; the telephone equipment, the existing stocks; even the central heating radiators had been bartered at the corner pub for cheese, ham and other commodities sold by his wife with the complicity of her lover, a German Feldwebel.

I quickly assessed the damage. Needless to say, my interview with Buchois rapidly turned into a violent quarrel. I dismissed him without further ado. He left, slamming the door and uttering threats. Two hours later, he was back and entered my office without knocking. He once again began to yell at me.

'You pretend that you've come from Bordeaux. That you'd lost your memory? Nonsense! Here is the proof.'

Reeling from too many drinks, his mouth distorted into a sneer, he flung an International Red Cross post-card on to the table. This type of card, with help from neutral countries, was the only link between the sealed frontiers of a world at war.

The brown card bore the London postmark and also the German Zenzur eagle. Its three printed headings read:

Person sought	:	Frédéric Lionel
Last seen	:	Gibraltar
Signature	:	Godot

The ceiling seemed to crash upon my head. Before the fall of Paris, Godot had worked with Buchois. I guessed what had happened. On his arrival in London, Godot started looking for me. He probably tried hard to find me, knocking at every possible door, without success. Encouraged — possibly — by Heidi equally eager to know more of my whereabouts, he took this absurd step hoping that Buchois might know how to get in touch with me. He was but too right.

Sitting in front of Buchois, I remained silent. I was entirely at his mercy. For a long minute, we stared at each other. Godot's stupid blunder had placed a sword of Damocles over my head. The slightest idea of revenge in Buchois' mind, and my fate was sealed.

Minutes passed, each one an eternity. What was he thinking? I shall never know. Suddenly he stood up and left without a word or gesture, leaving behind the compromising postcard.

Fear submerged me. Who can boast of never having been subjected to the sickening impact of it?

Courage may overcome fear, unconsciousness may conjure it, but it exists at all levels of consciousness, ranging from the fear of the unknown to the fear of not being able to enjoy quickly and to the full the pleasures of existence, the fear of growing old, of becoming sick, and of dying.

I have often known fear, especially of torture, and I have also been afraid of being afraid. It is a strange sensation, responsible for feverish and thoughtless actions.

Sometimes I managed to conquer fear, to go beyond it. Such

exceptional moments lead to adeptship giving one control over one's destiny.

Buchois did not betray me. After the war, I wanted to thank him for his silence but I heard he had died of delirium tremens. I still wonder what motivated his behaviour.

It might have been patriotism exacerbated by his wife's German lover. Did this fact drive him to become a drunkard? Very often drunkards talk wildly and boast... How could he conceal my secret from his wife?

Yet he took the secret with him to his grave. I owe him much. If it is true that we are called to have other experiences elsewhere, I shall be given the opportunity to show my gratitude.

In the course of this first exhausting day, I dealt first with the most pressing matters. I went to the police station to report the loss of my identity papers. For obvious reasons, the original ones had been left in London.

'What about your military papers?' asked the police superintendent who knew me by name.

'I have my demobilisation certificate,' I lied. 'But I did not bring it with me.'

My self-confidence was convincing. He gave me a voucher to serve in the event of a check. To go around as Henri Jonquière in Paris was out of the question. On the other hand, to establish my true identity whilst being able to use the other would be greatly to my advantage.

The same evening, feeling an urgent need to relax, I decided to have a drink at the Champclos, a fashionable establishment near the Etoile which I used to frequent before the war.

The place was crowded. The hubbub, the grey green uniforms, and the soft lights had a numbing effect on me. Maurice — the owner — welcomed me warmly and asked no questions. The artificial atmosphere, the blaring news broadcast every hour by the German High Command, seemed so remote from everything I had encountered lately; I just let myself float along with it.

I drank a lot of champagne, clinking glasses with my neighbours, savouring the relief of being my old self again. A light haze due to the wine dimmed the reality of recent events. Buchois, too, was losing substance, his threats had dissolved into a pink cloud. While I was smiling blissfully, somebody pressed my arm.

'Henri! What a surprise!', exclaimed a voice I knew.

Tania Borzareff, lovely in a pale grey suit, smiled down at me.

'Come and have dinner with us in the next room. I didn't care for your sudden disappearance from Lisbon without leaving an address. You will have to explain.'

Although very friendly, her words ended my short euphoria. I was faced with two alternatives; to vanish once and for all, or to admit that Tania, having discovered that I had used a false name, would draw obvious conclusions. These thoughts quickly sobered me. My mind started working at top speed. Could I try to make her, not my accomplice, but a confidant. A bold attempt, requiring also her husband's consent.

It was useless deceiving myself. The time for vital decisions had come.

I stammered an excuse and glanced towards the door, wondering if I could disappear into thin air. My wish was to cease to exist. Then, just as suddenly, I changed my mind.

Maybe the Buchois incident that morning had produced a delayed reaction, making me immune to unforeseen danger. Maybe, unconsciously, I believed that my guardian angel would not now forsake me.

The dark waters of the subconscious mind reflect abysmal impressions. Keyed-up to breaking point not long before, I regained total self-control. Taking both Tania's hands in mine, I explained how much I regretted a previous engagement, asking to be allowed to visit her the next day, wanting to see her alone, as I had important matters to communicate.

She mis-interpreted my words.

'You're certainly getting straight to the point', she answered smilingly. 'But if what you have to tell me is so interesting, do come tomorrow afternoon at four, rue Euler. We are staying there. My husband is out of town.'

With a last eloquent glance, she left to join her friends.

I returned to my apartment and paced up and down the corridor throughout the night. I kept telling myself that I should disappear, knowing that I would stay. It was my longest night. Morning found me a changed man. I had reached a state beyond fear.

Nothing is more difficult than to make it clear that to reach a state beyond fear is not merely an intellectual exercise; it consists of giving up beliefs and opinions to which one has been conditioned throughout one's life.

I fully accepted the possibility of death and the failure of my mission, and thanks to this acceptance my fear dissolved. My inner transformation early that morning enabled me to regard the havoc I had found at the factory as secondary. I took all the steps required to ensure its future. I visited various banks to obtain the loans badly needed to somehow keep going. I did everything a boss is supposed to do in trying to safeguard his business and the livelihood of his employees.

I reached Tania's home in the middle of the afternoon. What took place at this vital meeting is blurred in my memory.

I remember a vast, requisitioned impersonal apartment, soft lights, a Louis XVI clock ticking on the black marble mantelpiece; few other details. My emotional faculties had been overstrained. I had crossed a threshold beyond which one no longer participates in whatever happens.

I accepted the love affair as a logical outcome. But it altered the problem.

To be able to count Tania as an ally was marvellous luck, but it also entailed a dangerous dependence. Would she consent — upon learning what I could not hide from her — to 'cover an agent' of an enemy power? Would she want to let her husband into the secret? What would be his attitude if he began to suspect our relationship? As for Tania, a child spoilt by life, would she imagine that I had become her lover solely to save

77

myself, and if so, how would she react?

My mind was in a turmoil. I chain-smoked nervously to give myself time to think.

'What are you thinking about?' asked Tania tenderly. 'You seem so far away. Aren't you happy?'

The moment had come. I tried to make my words sound convincing, I explained that my use of a false name had been prompted by the desire to be repatriated, not to become an enemy agent.

'In Lisbon, I was Henri Jonquière. Here, in Paris, you must forget him. In London, I agreed to carry out a mission in order to return home. What else could I have done? I promised to do what they wanted. The stratagem I used is a secret we shall share and which will tighten the bonds that unite us. Who knows if one day, both you and your husband won't be glad to have proved by your silence that your collaboration with the New Europe did not exclude other sympathies. The world changes, and it is wiser to adopt a flexible attitude. In 1916, the Germans believed that they had won the war; in 1918, they were defeated.'

Deeply upset, Tania rejected all my arguments. In a state of tension, tossed between opposing loyalties, she cried out:

'Just imagine if Nicolas learns the truth. Suppose I accept your suggestions and tell him that Henri Jonquière was a false name and that the British Secret Service sent you to Paris in order to entice me into your arms. Nicolas isn't a fool. He'll kill us both with his own hands. You forget he is the Consul of a country allied to the Axis. Besides. . .' and she burst into tears.

I understood her feelings and did not insist. It was her own decision. I sensed a spontaneous tenderness in her outburst, and so I left without being too worried.

The next day she called me on the phone. On recognising my voice and without giving her name, she whispered:

'The one who has returned agrees. At least, for the time being. He will keep silent about what I told him. But I do not guarantee the future. I know I'm a fool, I'm bringing. . . Oh! How I hate you!' And she rang off.

The meeting with Tania and our intimacy radically altered the problems with which I was confronted.

As a double-faced Janus, I adopted two different personalities: the one taking part in the superficial whirl of Paris amusements; the other wracking his brain organising a network of safe-houses.

The first met Tania regularly at the Champclos. Patronising a fashionable cocktail bar was a plausible alibi for her frequent absences from home.

The second had made his headquarters in a bistro in a working class quarter of Paris, and it was from there that instructions were issued. Its owner, a friend of Albert's, established useful contacts, and the threads of a strong web of interconnections were gradually woven.

The Champclos was a favourite haunt of soldiers on the spree, and of young women seeking adventures. Agents on the lookout for information, black marketeers, and the usual pre-war patrons formed a cosmopolitan crowd against a background of victory bulletins and loudspeakers blaring out every half hour. Apparently carefree, they tried to blot out their worries.

Costly cigarettes, food, and addresses where to get this or that changed hands, while the ladies showed off extravagant fashions ill suited to the shortages of the times.

The contrast between the atmosphere of the bistro and the Champclos made me realise the increasingly wide cleavage between the spiritless and numb majority of the population and those believing, or feigning to believe in the miracle of the New Order, from which they might benefit.

Torn between opposing trends, a handful of men and women were preparing to fight a relentless struggle — the shadow fighters — members of the Resistance movement.

So much has been written about the Resistance, as well as collaboration with the victors, that details of my own experiences are superfluous.

To stick to the essentials of the story, I need to mention the incredible resourcefulness of those who contributed in setting up and strengthening the Line, the name we gave to our infiltration and exfiltration network — professional terms which are self-explanatory.

During this period of contrasting darkness and light, I had the good fortune to be at an observation post with antennae in three worlds:

First, the incongruous world of the occupied territory, consisting of all kinds of opportunists, of more or less willing allies, visionaries and politicians won over because they believed — sometimes quite sincerely — that they could in the long run rid the country of the Germans.

Second, the Resistance movement, at first almost absent but gradually gaining strength despite internal dissensions; and finally, the so-called free world, the countries fighting against the Axis.

As I passed from the world of collaboration to that of resistance and from there to the free world outside the fortress of Europe, I was able to understand how propaganda convinced those enclosed in each that their cause was the only just one.

In France, a *modus vivendi* had established itself, notwithstanding or because of the ubiquitous and well-organised moral tension supported by ruthless police forces.

On the one hand, the sweeping German victories in Russia, the systematic looting of industries and art treasures, the desire for survival of which the Black Market was only one aspect; on the other, the London broadcasts, the echoes of the Resistance's deeds, still sporadic, but daily becoming more obvious, plus the ever more improbable invasion of the British Isles, explain the confusion reigning in people's minds. They also showed the ineffectiveness of collaboration trumpeted everywhere as a success.

Magnified and distorted by contradictions, the news coming from Europe and the outside world influenced public opinion in every way.

Few really committed themselves to take sides, and this lack of decision hampered my task considerably as I had to be doubly careful in my recruitment.

London had sent me a pianist, and after his arrival the

connection with the Service was firmly established. Through him weekly exchanges of messages became possible. In addition, the valuable co-operation of a railwayman working at La Tour de Carol, a village near the Spanish border, made it possible to pass documents to the other side.

Under growing pressure, the European stronghold was becoming accustomed to war. Standpoints were ventilated, protestations of faith and high-sounding statements were made, measures ensuring the submission born of fear were taken. Meanwhile, hunger was spreading, increasing the general hardship and confusion. Some just accepted, others hoped, a few decided to fight. Only clear-minded men understood that the world-scale confrontation constituted a challenge launched by fanatics with a power philosophy, opposed — so they said — to the degradation due to traditional humanism, an obsolete ideal of a world bound to decay.

Tania tried, not very convincingly, to make me share this view. She was not the only one. Other friends did their best to prove the advantages of total allegiance, not only to Marshal Pétain's policy, considered too timorous, but to the New Europe concept, a vision of a radiant future promised in the event of a German victory.

'Look at this military parade', said one of them one day on the Champs-Elysées. 'This is not a circus. It's a parade of men convinced of their supremacy. Go and listen to George Claude's lectures. He is a scientist of world renown. The arguments he develops are absolutely convincing.'

In flashy night-clubs the hubbub of artificial gaiety and the noise of gypsy bands drowned the echoes of distress, hiding the lack of heating, hot water and hope. 'Traitors Shot at Dawn', proclaimed blood-red posters. 'Enlist in the French Volunteers' Legion and destroy international communism', urged the newspapers. 'Follow the Marshal', enjoined the propaganda. 'Listen to the BBC', whispered the patriots. 'Students Rebel', head-lined the underground press. Everybody distrusted everybody, as informers became more numerous and spared nobody.

81

'European' gatherings warmly welcomed high-ranking officers of the occupying armies, Axis diplomats and heads of missions, as well as the French who wished to be in the wind.

Small, intimate parties were organised, even psychic sessions, leaving the task of advising mortals to the spirits. Tania and Nicolas assiduously attended them, and took me to one shortly after our first meeting at the Champclos.

Tania had even confided that the spirits had advised the couple to remain on friendly terms with me, understandable since Tania had won the medium's sympathy.

Nicolas was a man of complex character, and ambitious. He thought his wife to be a major asset in his climb to power. Having lived in London, he did not share the certainty of an Axis victory; he had agreed to keep silent about my past as a guarantee for the future, should the Axis lose the war.

Tania was intelligent, sensual, with a delightful voice. She knew how to charm her hosts, whenever necessary; her interest in occult sciences strengthened her illusion that she belonged to a circle of psychic initiates in the upper regions of National Socialism.

The so-called leading personalities who had surfaced on the wave of the Axis armies' advance took advantage of every opportunity to celebrate the New Europe. One day, a Russian bastion having fallen to the Wehrmacht, Tania phoned me. Being afraid that her telephone might be bugged, she never mentioned her husband's name. This sort of game added spice to our quite harmless conversation.

'The-one-you-know wants me to accompany him this evening to Madame So and So. Lots of friends will be present. Our Armies have won a great victory. You must come too and celebrate their success.'

Sensing my hesitation, she added that a refusal would grieve her terribly. Unthinkingly, she was taking advantage of a situation already sufficiently complicated, my underground activities frequently requiring long absences which my pretty mistress dreaded. She lost no chance of showing her strong displeasure at having to endure my so-called business trips.

The Line indeed was in operation. We now had four safe-houses. To start with only airmen and agents on special missions parachuted over enemy territory were given the password to these. Once accepted, the 'customer' was conveyed step-by-step to a safe-house on the Mediterranean coast for embarkation on a submarine or small vessel camouflaged as a fishing boat. The risks incurred in crossing the country were enormous. The members of the Line escorted the parcels from one safe-house to another, and finally to the Villa Isabelle in Cannes, the last stop before embarkation.

Tania, of course, knew nothing of this. Not wishing to upset her, I accepted the invitation.

The idea that a 'dreadful terrorist' could penetrate into this circle tickled my sense of humour. Therefore, not too un-willingly I joined the Borzareffs and we made our way together to the Avenue Mozart.

The reception was in full swing. Nothing was lacking, neither delicious food nor vintage wines. At a propitious moment, a well-known Parisian stock-broker requested silence for a toast:

'I raise my glass to the Wehrmacht and its gallant Allies. May they achieve a final victory and crush the supporters of plutocracy which has harmed us so greatly.'

A businessman followed him:

'Only Germany can save us from the Bolshevik curse. Should the Anglo-Saxon forces ever dare land on French soil, I shall take up arms to help drive them out.'

Was it merely a vain boast? Maybe! Nevertheless, I met the same businessman soon after the Liberation in the uniform of the Free French.

Everybody raised their glasses. I did the same, but I could not drink. My throat was dry.

'Aren't you drinking, Mr. Lionel?'

The question was asked by a Transylvanian, manager of two Paris music-halls expropriated because formerly owned by Jews.

I had become the centre of attention; Nicolas was looking at me ironically, Tania fearfully, the others in surprise.

It was extremely embarrassing, I glanced mechanically at an autographed photograph on the wall behind the buffet. It was of a young woman in a skin-tight garment practicing a sport called Rhön-Rad — a kind of wheel formed by two rims linked to each other by cross-bars. The exercise consisted in making the wheel turn, while clutching the cross-bars with both hands, the feet tightly fixed to others.

On the photograph, a caption was engraved in gold letters. It said: 'The wheel turns'. Its meaning and its possible *double entendre* overwhelmed me. I couldn't utter a word. I stood as if hypnotized. All eyes followed mine.

The silence was complete.

'An angel is passing', exclaimed a German general, the boss of show-business in occupied France, breaking the tension which could have ended in my arrest. I sighed with relief while he looked at me. I am positive that I detected a glimmer of sympathy in his glance. What were his true feelings? I guessed them while the hubbub broke out again. He knew the wheel was indeed turning.

I want to give an overall impression of the atmosphere of that period as experienced by someone whose perilous situation compelled him to bypass personal considerations. The Line was functioning and, more than once, ingenuity had to compensate for deficiencies. From the outset, crossing the demarcation line posed a thorny problem, both for us and for the parcels.

I solved this difficulty in an unexpected way. I had to return to Sete to ask Secco to find out whether the owners of the *Aurora* — Peter and Costa — might co-operate. Their ship, anchored in port, could be of use some day. It was just an idea, but it had to be followed up.

I wanted Fernand's advice first, and I left for Marseille.

This was yet another business trip which exasperated Tania.

A farmer whom I knew took me across the heavily-guarded border, and we were almost captured by a patrol. Luckily we escaped detection, but once again it brought home to us the huge risks involved.

Except for a stronghold such as the Berlin wall, any frontier is more or less vulnerable. The border line separating the so-called free zone from the occupied was well guarded, but was no exception to this principle.

The people, arbitrarily separated by the will of the occupying forces, knew each other. They were familiar with every fold of the ground, and through the sheer necessity of repetition, the watch rounds became a matter of routine and could, therefore, to a certain extent be foreseen.

The so-called ferrymen took great risks in helping clandestine travellers voluntarily, or for remuneration. Imprisonment, deportation and confiscation of their property were the punishments inflicted.

The one I contacted had twice helped some of our parcels to cross, but even so he was reluctant and very careful.

I found him on his farm, not far from the Cher river, which we were supposed to cross by boat, sunk in a dead arm of the river under some willow branches. At about two a.m. on a blissful pitch-dark night we bailed the water as quickly as possible out of the flat-bottomed barge. The German military police patrolled both banks of the river, and we spent some time waiting, lying on the ground behind a flock of sheep grouped round the ram. His legs had been tied by the ferryman so as to immobilise him during the passing of the patrol, who had a couple of dogs on the leash.

The scent of the sheep stifled ours, and as soon as the sound of the patrol had faded away, we dashed to the river. We crossed without mishap. But once on the other side things went wrong.

We had hardly touched the bank when bullets whizzed above our heads. We wasted no time.

Without hesitation and with every bit of our strength, the ferryman pulling the oars and I pushing with a pole, we moved off, seeking to make use of the current in the middle of the river in order to escape.

It had begun to rain, lightning streaked the sky, and we could be seen now and again as if floodlit. In addition, a searchlight scanned the water trying to catch us in its beam. We rowed and pushed for life. A bend of the river protected us for a moment just as the searchlight, mounted on a truck, which had caught up with us on the other side of the river, spotted us. In haste we ran aground and took to our heels.

We ran straight ahead. I stumbled, fell, got up again, ran again. The rain was falling thick and fast. In the distance shouts and barks were audible. The ferryman had disappeared. Panting, I kept on as fast as I could.

Mud bespattered, soaked to the skin, lost, I moved forward. The instinct of survival is immensely powerful. I crossed a road and plunged into a wood and banged against a wooden shack. I dodged in and, exhausted, sank to the ground.

My fate was in God's hands. Once more He protected me. The torrential rain had washed out my trail. Shivering, I waited for daylight. When it came I left my shelter, walked to a road, kept well into the hedge and moved to what I thought was the South.

A sign-post pointing to the opposite direction made my heart drum: Saint Forent sur Cher — 8km. I was well and truly in the free zone and for the time being out of immediate danger.

As soon as I arrived in Marseille, I hurried to Fernand. He advised me to avoid Secco who was under surveillance since the Secretary General's arrest. He dissuaded me from approaching Peter, whose brother, Costa, had been taken into custody for reasons unknown.

'These two people are adventurers', he stated. 'True, they are Greeks and their country's fate probably makes them sympathisers. But their greed is dangerous. It brought them back to France in the hope of finding other diamond merchants to fleece. They were wrong. The friends they relied upon may have changed sides, and the *Aurora* is now under embargo. Forget it!'

I did so. That same evening, sitting in the waiting-room of the Saint Charles railway station, waiting for the Paris train, indefinitely delayed, I day-dreamed. Next to me a strong young man was dozing. I learnt later that he was a railwayman returning to Chalon-sur-Saône, his home station.

An individual with a hang-dog look sat in front of us, and pulled us both out of our torpor. After two or three vain attempts to start a conversation, he got up, came closer and bent down to whisper in our ears:

'The British will shortly be landing in Normandy. All true patriots must be told. Pass the news on to others. We must be ready. The time for revenge is drawing near.'

The railwayman's face brightened; he was just about to say something when I kicked him under the bench. Undoubtedly, the individual was an *agent provocateur* and this kind of approach was part of a method for trapping fools. It was only too obvious.

It took a few seconds before the railwayman understood his blunder. He gulped and shrugging his shoulders muttered:

'I couldn't care less!' adding: 'If the English try, they'll be sitting ducks, and it'll serve them right.'

I enforced this statement energetically.

The man realised that sincere or not we would not budge from our position, and went away disgruntled.

The railwayman later that night thanked me, and the mutual confidence was established. We started talking. He was the one to suggest a brilliantly simple scheme for crossing the zone border. I tested its reliability the very next time.

That day, I was escorting four Belgians. Hitch-hiking on a truck of the Ministry of Supplies, we reached Dijon. From there we took a bus to Chalon-sur-Saône, where our railway man friend, true to his word, was waiting for us at the terminal.

He led us to a lampman's hut wedged between two tracks about one hundred metres from the station. One should understand that Chalon was a border town with the river forming the demarcation line.

Hidden in the hut, we waited until nightfall. Through the single window-pane, begrimed by years of accumulated dust, I kept watch for the train from Mâcon, that is from the Free

Zone, which we wished to enter. It was due at eleven p.m. German time.

Numerous workers from a power station located on the free bank of the river used this train, their homes being in the Occupied North Zone. They naturally owned an *Ausweis*, the pass enabling them to get to their job.

A distant clock chimed eleven. A whistle blew. The train was entering the station. The time to act had come. We left the hut without haste. Walking silently in Indian file, we approached the platform along which the train had stopped, crossing the rails as we went. In the blackout we could not make out the flow of passengers leaving the coaches on their way towards the staircase leading to the German check-point at the other end of the underground corridor. Two soldiers with tommy-guns faced the train in order to make sure that no passenger could bypass the staircase in the centre of the platform. Their instructions were to keep a close watch on the passengers. What happened behind their backs was not their concern.

We were therefore able to get close without being spotted. Moving quickly, we slipped into the throng of passengers as far away as possible from the two soldiers. The risk of being noticed was slight as this stratagem had apparently no logical purpose.

The passengers went through the check-point one by one. Finally it was our turn.

While handing over five forged identity cards to the lieutenant sitting behind a table, I said:

'Sir, we've just arrived from Mâcon and we have no *Ausweis*. I pointed my finger to the four motionless Belgians behind me. We were told that we could enter the Occupied Zone for twenty four hours without an *Ausweis*, and I'd like....'

'*Nix Ausweis. Retour*', he thundered, interrupting me and handing back the identity cards. 'Wagner!' An NCO appeared and saluted, clicking his heels. 'Wagner, escort these un-disciplined Frenchmen to a waiting-room, lock them up until the train from Paris arrives and send them all back!'

This was just what we had hoped for. Behind locked doors in a musty office at midnight, we saw the express train from Paris entering the station. We knew that a systematic search was sparing nothing and nobody. We caught a glimpse of two unfortunate devils flanked by policemen in civilian clothes being pushed out of the train and disappear into the darkness.

One hour passed, and then another.

'Let's hope they won't search our kit', muttered one of my parcels with a strong Limbourg accent. 'The documents I carry are dynamite!'

I didn't answer. The whole escape mechanism was geared to the predictable behaviour of men strictly obeying precise instructions without any personal initiative. As we were to be sent back from where we had supposedly come, we did not belong to the category of people subjected to being searched. And blind obedience indeed triumphed.

A few minutes before the train's departure, Wagner and another chap made us climb into the packed coaches, completely disregarding the suitcases we were carrying.

Wagner and his comrade were watching us closely. Trying to make his French understandable, he honoured me with a sharp comment:

'Nix D system with us. Understood?'

D stands for the French *debrouiller*, meaning resourcefulness.

The train rumbled towards the Free Zone. If Wagner is still alive and by chance these lines come his way, he will learn that the D system operated throughout the war, for even after both zones were occupied the demarcation line remained closely watched.

The only essential precaution we had to take was to ascertain that at every fresh crossing recently transferred members of the Gestapo had replaced the former ones who might remember our stratagem.

Thanks to the instructions applied to the letter and to the holy regulations, we succeeded on one memorable attempt in getting twelve parcels sent back under similar circumstances. To be sent back meant to be sent to the Free Zone with the benediction and the help of the occupying forces, and without being checked. The Germans were so convinced of the superiority of discipline, that to them resourcefulness was nothing more than a Latin vice.

11

Comic and serious incidents, acts of bravery and of cowardice, moments of great joy or intense weariness, moral and physical misery highlighted by periods of deep calm, tumble over each other in my memory.

For various reasons, I had informed the Service of my relationship with Tania. I had explained that it helped to foster social contacts providing good cover for clandestine activities. To prevent workers from being sent to Germany, I was struggling hard to keep the plant open without producing anything more than trifles.

Dereck, to make me realise that my explanations did not impress him, humourously changed my code name in messages intended for me on the 'French Speak to the French' broadcasts from London to 'Rudolph Valentino'.

My comrades and I listened daily whenever possible to these badly jammed broadcasts, keeping our ears wide open so as not to miss one of those vital messages.

A simple code indicated the town where we could expect a parcel. This enabled us to send one of our friends to the safe-house, to take charge and watch over the step-by-step convoy to the Mediterranean shore.

Many setbacks occurred during this period and great was the bravery and self-denial of all those who worked for the Line. Fortunately, only a few sacrificed their freedom, but some paid with their lives.

The 1942 summer was fading into autumn. Two events and

their consequences hastened my decision to return to London. The Service approved wholeheartedly, believing that the head of an escape net-work should not tempt fortune for too long.

This attitude bothered me as I did not want to be retained in England for security reasons. Nevertheless, I decided to take the first opportunity to return to Perfidious Albion — as the French press called Great Britain — after more than two years absence.

I looked forward very much to seeing my children again, and I also wished to make them fully aware on the other side of the Channel of the subtle changes taking place in the mentality of the population in metropolitan France.

The occupying power and the French who had gambled on its victory were slowly losing their arrogance. Ruthless reprisals were often blindly taken against 'terrorists' whose actions, it must be admitted, were often bungled.

Paris, a web of intrigues, deals and counter-deals, prey to all kinds of speculators, the dream city for soldiers on leave from the Russian front was changing sides. To the superficial observer, everything was as usual. Traffic was almost nil, the subway packed, the food queues longer than ever, prices sky-high at the de luxe restaurants not subjected to rationing and reserved for the victors.

The change was in the people's eyes. Utter weariness and endless fear could be read in their faces, of the police, of the Gestapo, of being sent to Germany, of lacking food, of vainly waiting for a prisoner's return, of seeing a relative disappear without trace — so many fearful things. Nevertheless, hope was rising. Yesterday's victor imperceptibly was becoming tomorrow's loser in their minds.

The first of the two events I have just referred to happened about that time. I met Colonel Alric and his mistress, both members of a Resistance movement.

I had agreed — at my friend Bernard's request — to make their acquaintance, although for security reasons I generally avoided any direct contact with other underground organisations.

Colonel Alric was an ambitious man. He wanted to submit to General de Gaulle a precise layout to unify all existing groups, an idea that the Chief of Free France apparently advocated. He therefore asked me to arrange his departure. I asked London for their approval and without any explanation received a negative reply.

Alric, very angry, told me at length about his plans. I offered to take a report to England if he would prepare one.

I knew about his activities and was impressed by his precise views on the general situation as well as by his mistress's courage. She had not hesitated, in spite of great personal risk, to plunge into the river Cher in order to escape pursuit by the enemy.

As I badly wanted to cross into the Free Zone to take a rest in a house I owned at Amphion on Lake Geneva, I suggested to Alric that I should meet him just before my embarkation on the Mediterranean coast, and we fixed an appointment at the Villa Isabelle, our safe-house operating in Cannes.

Shortly after this interview, I informed Tania of my intention of taking a vacation in my home in Savoy.

'I've just seen a doctor. One of my lungs is slightly affected. It is not serious, but I need mountain air for two months.'

Although she raised no objections, I knew she felt upset.

Possessing a perfect *Ausweis* forged in the South Zone, I decided to travel just for once by sleeper. Manifestly an imprudence and a sign that I was getting too cocky.

'I'm leaving for a few days rest at home', I told my friend Bernard. 'Why not come along?'

We were both having a drink at the Champclos, and my suggestion clearly attracted him.

'Why not indeed? Particularly as I promised Alric, who left a few days ago, to hand him some documents in Marseille. Alas! I have no *Ausweis* and time is short. Maybe...'

He called Maurice, the barman and drew him aside.

'You told me about a man who forges *Ausweise*. Is he reliable?'

Maurice reassured him.

'He'll get you one more genuine than the real thing.'

He grinned broadly.

'How much will it cost?' asked Bernard.

'Ten pounds of butter', said Maurice. 'Freddy, the hairdresser in the Lido passage has just received some. Tell him I sent you, but hurry.'

A few days later, we took the train. At Chalon-sur-Saône, two German Gestapo officers opened the door of our sleeper to check our papers. Mine was returned after close scrutiny, but Bernard was not so lucky. Carefully examining his *Ausweis*, one officer said to the other in German.

'It's a forgery.'

Asking again for mine — which was equally false, he peered at it through his magnifying glass and handing it back, stated:

'This one is genuine, the other is not.'

Both went away and returned with two plain-clothes policemen. They ransacked our luggage, but did not suspect me. I managed to hide the documents under my blankets, which Bernard had passed on to me, guessing that his journey was over.

Arrested, he left the compartment without a gesture. I hardly slept the rest of the night and blamed myself for disregarding the elementary rules of the game.

It is time to correct a false impression which the reader might have received.

It might be imagined that I always tackled events like a hero without fear.

Nothing could be more unfounded. I had, of course, become accustomed to danger. I was able under exceptional circumstances to unfold myself, becoming a witness of the scene in which I was playing a part, freed from blinding instinctive and passionate impulses.

But the being within, nevertheless, reacted at times and then paralysing fear invaded me. The happenings in the train are a perfect example.

How, I asked myself, can unbelievable luck be explained? How was it that a forged *Ausweis* compared with another forged

Ausweis had been accepted as genuine without any additional checking?

Such luck could not last! Sooner or later I should be caught.

Fortune is a capricious Goddess. She could abandon me tomorrow, in an hour, at the next check-point. My temples were throbbing. I was drenched in sweat.

'Give up before it is too late', insinuated the creature within myself. 'Torture will be yours. Death is nothing, but what about the appalling pain. Are you prepared to endure it?'

'No!' it howled back, evoking memories of events which could have ended in disaster. It was not hard to remember the incident with the two Abwehr fellows of the counter-espionage who succeeded in worming their way into the Line.

Their dubious behaviour betrayed them. They were kept under surveillance day and night, and they were despatched before they realised it to whatever fate awaited them in England.

Had they been less conscientious, less persevering, wishing to follow the chain to the last link, relying on their false Belgian identity, they could have vanished beforehand, then I and all the others of the Line would now have been swinging on the gallows.

'I was lucky again, but my luck is running out. The closing of the safe-house, the pass word of which was probably extorted by the Abwehr from an RAF chap, offers no guarantee. They will get you in the long run', whispered the creature within.

And panic-stricken, it suggested back to itself:

'Speed up your departure for London. Drop Alric. His Marseille lair is almost certainly being watched.'

Thoughts were chasing thoughts; all were sombre. Long, very long, are the hours under such conditions. The train bumped ahead and, at each stop, the possibility of sudden arrest awaited me.

Slowly I emerged. My task remained unfinished. I had to complete it. Abandon yourself to a Reality beyond was Garcia's recommendation. I tried hard, knowing that it was the only way to transcend the most human of instinctive reactions, the fear of death.

94

At Marseille I handed over to Alric the set of documents Bernard had entrusted me with.

Then I left for Amphion, planning to stay merely two days before returning to Paris to warn Bernard's friends.

As manager of a large company, with no earlier difficulties, his offence was merely an attempt to cross the demarcation line illegally. I hoped he might get off with three months' imprisonment. Nevertheless, it was better to lose no time.

My house in Amphion set amid majestic trees on the edge of the lake is a haven of serenity. As I sat on a bollard I kept glancing enviously at the Swiss shore — so near and yet so far. It was inconceivable! On the other side, peace reigned. A few miles separated order from disorder, legality from violence, torture and death.

I remembered the large white boats that in peace time passed to and fro in front of the house with their red paddle wheels reflecting the rays of the sun.

The yellow and rust-coloured leaves on the plane trees bordering the lake heralded autumn. What did the coming year hold in store? What new sufferings?

Lost in my thoughts, I heard footsteps, and turning round saw to my immense amazement, Tania. She flung herself into my arms.

'I'm with you for good', she murmured, her eyes radiant.

'I'll never leave you again! I can't bear it when you are away. We'll be happy. I love you. Nicolas understands, he accepts the situation and does not want to stand in the way of my happiness. Tell me you are happy, please.'

What could I say? What could I do? First I had to calm her; drastic measures were needed before it was too late.

'However did you get here?' I asked, more annoyed than I wished to appear.

'Oh! Very easily. Nicolas is a dear! He let me have the Embassy car with the driver. I didn't even have time to send him away. I saw you sitting here and rushed down. The driver is waiting for orders in front of the house. Tell him where to sleep tonight. He'll drive back tomorrow morning.'

'With us', I said firmly. 'Do you want me alive or dead?'

Her eyes filled with tears.

'You are rejecting me!'

'Tania', I insisted, 'don't be so impulsive. Just think for a minute. Nicolas is ambitious. Being fond of you, he has made a gesture which sooner or later he'll regret. Let's wait for the end of this war. It's crazy to endanger our future before that. Be sensible!'

As if to support my words, a boy on a bicycle approached.

'A telegram for Mr. Frédéric Lionel.'

I opened it. It came from Vichy and was signed Nicolas. The few grandiloquent but menacing words read: 'Give me back my wife or I'll crush you like a fly.'

Bombastic, but an unmistakeable threat.

'Is Nicolas in Vichy?'

'Yes', quavered Tania. 'We went there together, but he is returning to Paris this evening.'

The rest of the day was spent arguing passionately.

Finally, Tania surrendered.

'We'll return to Paris tomorrow. We'll see Nicolas, who seems willing to forgive and forget. Let us part until the end of hostilities. We may then decide about our future. Maybe I'll be able to prove my gratitude to you both. I am now convinced of a German defeat.'

We left by car the next day. It was not a cheerful journey. I met Nicolas with Tania at a café in the Place Péreire. He behaved calmly and did not blame his wife, at least not in my presence. However, he did mention that he might need my help one day and that I should not forget his present generosity.

It was a narrow escape and more than ever I wished to turn my back upon danger and visit the other side which I imagined to be pure and beautiful.

12

A creek at Cape Aiguillon, a dark night and a cold drizzle. Four chilly figures including mine crouched by the water, an exchange of light signals, a boat being beached into which we silently huddled, hands held out to drag us on board a tiny Royal Navy vessel. That was the stage-setting of our clandestine departure for Gibraltar.

Mechanical trouble delayed us. The engine kept backfiring, and two of the crew bustled about without any tangible result.

Overwhelming feelings gripped me: the fear of a possible last-minute failure, exuberant joy at having succeeded so far in escaping the traps scattered on my path, and pride in having helped to save lives.

Crazy thoughts whirled through my head, and mad ideas criss-crossed in my brain. But hope remained.

I believe my companions experienced the same impressions while listening to the noise of the engine threatening to ruin our escape.

Suddenly, out of the darkness, a deep voice hailed us:

'For God's sake, clear off! A German frigate is making straight for you!' The young woman whose voice I recognised as Germaine Sablon's, a popular singer, was already rowing hastily away. (I take this opportunity to pay a belated homage to her courage).

The time seemed endless before we could put to sea. And although no German craft challenged us, we knew we had had a narrow escape.

Gibraltar in war-time! Imagine a main street, crossing the town from one end to the other, crowded to capacity with soldiers of every race and all services. A main street without one civilian, since all Spaniards working in the city had to leave the Rock every evening, their homes being mostly on the other side of the bay. Liquor flowed in torrents, the innumerable bars and

97

pubs being literally taken by assault. Military police wearing white helmets tried to keep order, using their sticks when necessary, while bawdy songs and martial tunes drowned out every other noise.

We dined at the Officers' Mess where the walls were covered with bull-fight posters.

'Let's go and have fun', suggested the captain detailed to look after me. This meant drinking here and drinking there, meeting Jim, Jack, Jerry on the way from one pub to another.

The music, if you dare call it that — was ear-splitting. Mechanical pianos, accordians. 'Swing' on tinny gramophones. Some men were singing, others dancing, nearly all ending up blind drunk. A sad joy this drowning of sorrow in drink to create the illusion of gaiety, and at the cost of a monstrous hang-over.

More clearly in Gibraltar than anywhere else did I fully comprehend the emptiness produced by the absence of usual occupations or professions. An emptiness that could certainly be better filled in awakening human interests other than drink and sex.

We stayed in Gibraltar for a few days. A Flying Fortress took us to London.

To breathe the air of the British capital gave me wings. The lacerating oppression of every instant was replaced by joyous relief at having nothing to fear. Whereas in France the omnipresent and omnipotent grey-green uniforms raised apprehension, the sight of the allied uniforms was sheer delight. The change of scenery seemed almost unreal, and I sometimes thought I was the victim of a mirage. As the crow flies, the Champs-Elysées was quite near Piccadilly; in fact they were a world apart.

'Go to the police station', suggested the Service officer who met me at the airport. 'I have prepared identity papers in the name of Durand for you and a landing certificate stamped by the Patriotic School, a sorting centre for refugees. There we try to discover the true motives of those who arrive, and God help the spies hidden in the crowds of those joining us to fight the enemy. You are supposed to be a French refugee. It would be wise to take precautions to jumble any track you may have left. Act as if you were Durand. Never forget that you are going back and that, notwithstanding our efforts, enemy eyes are everywhere. At the police station you will be issued with a temporary identity card and a ration book. Nobody must think during your stay here that you are not that fine chap Durand who has come to fight in our ranks.'

'And if I meet friends?'

'Stay at home, don't show yourself. Your life is at stake, not mine. The best lie is the one you are not forced to tell.'

To carry out the formalities, I reported to the nearest police station off Regent Street. There I faced by sheer chance the Inspector who, on my previous arrival, had issued my identity papers in the name of Frédéric Lionel. I recognised him at once but did not think that he would remember me. I was wrong. He left for a few minutes and I suddenly found myself flanked by two determined gentlemen ushering me into a small room. There, the white-haired inspector asked me sternly to explain my dual identity. It wasn't difficult. A telephone call cleared it up. But I could not help congratulating the Inspector, although he might have felt disappointed at not having collared a dangerous spy.

This task done, I hastened to visit my daughters. They greeted me as a stranger. Both had adopted as theirs the family to whom I had entrusted them. They even refused to speak French, as they had suffered intensely from being different from their playmates.

Although they did not quite know whether they ought to be glad or not, I promised to come back as often as possible, before leaving again for other shores.

In London, I walked the streets, enjoying to the full the sensation of being able to move freely and talk without fear, to be, in fact, on the right side of the fence.

The air-raids had caused havoc since my last stay: ruins, charred walls, gaping façades marred the whole city. However, life seemed to be going on normally. Boards at the entrance of shops with smashed windows announced Business as Usual.

Servicemen of all ranks and from allied nations filled the streets. The cold determination of 1940 had given way to the certainty of victory. Consequently, the spirit of competition inciting men — even when allied — to try to be the first to reach the winning-post, could be felt in words and writings.

To enjoy life, to have the police as accomplices and one's conscience at peace, made me euphoric. One evening, casting caution to the winds, I went to the French Club. I just couldn't help it, I had been looking forward to this moment for too long.

The atmosphere was animated. My travelling companion, a Socialist member of Parliament, was addressing the audience, which included the film stars Françoise Rosay and Claude Dauphin, and numerous members of the French colony in London. The speaker's eloquence — very much in the Third Republic style — kindled general enthusiasm. That evening the French Club in St. James' Square represented the home-land; the tearful audience responded with frenzied patriotism to the vibrant words uttered by a man who had just escaped from his country, crushed under the enemy's heel.

Françoise and Claude took the floor in turn, and the huge ovation that greeted the end of each speech culminated in everybody singing the *Marseillaise*. The last note had hardly died away, when a dignified gentleman requested silence.

'Dear fellow countrymen', said Gaston Palewski solemnly, 'to my great sorrow not one of you has once uttered the name of our providential leader, de Gaulle. Although I do not think it was done on purpose, I must point out this oversight. I therefore ask you to close this meeting in order to give you time to think things over and make good your omission the next time. Dear countrymen, I look forward to meeting you again, provided, of course that you fully understand why your attitude was disturbing.'

Silence fell. The audience left. The shock I experienced was the more severe as it was unexpected. Coming from a world ruled by terror, I had thought to reach a free, united world. To be so brutally deceived upset a whole set of ideas to which I was attached. In France, party politics were obsolete. But here, they again imposed their rule on men and women who had dared to forget them.

From that evening onward the glamour of the London universe paled. There was a yawning gap between reality and my shattered illusions.

Two days later, I had another unpleasant experience. In an office in Carlton Gardens, I met high ranking officials of the Free French Forces. We made a complete survey of the situation and I tried to give them useful information about the psychological warfare they wished to continue. I quickly realised that their outlook distorted the problems. They divided the French citizens between good and bad with nothing in between. The former were those devoted to their cause, the latter everyone else. When I attempted to enlighten them, they smiled indulgently as if deploring my innocent simplicity.

'In your opinion, what is the impact of our French broadcasts by the BBC?' asked one official.

I hesitated before answering.

'Attack Darlan, Laval, Henriot and others, but spare Pétain. For many Frenchmen, plunged into the horror of defeat, he remains victor of Verdun, the flag-bearer of France; his pictures are encircled by the three French colours, the only ones to be seen in occupied territory. For many they symbolise France eternal.'

It was no doubt a big blunder. My words sparked off a general uproar. I was risking being labelled a bad citizen, although I was only striving to explain the behaviour adapted to circumstances, on one side of the Channel, but regarded as criminal on the other.

I returned home in a thoughtful mood.

It was in London that I lost the illusions I had harboured until then. Obviously, wisdom was not the foundation guiding those in power on both sides of the Channel, and its absence distressed me.

I was living in a room rented from a French lady in a house in Hammersmith. There were two other tenants: Josiane, the young widow of an airman who had just been shot down, and Nadia, a Pole, who was leaving for an unknown destination.

We gathered in the evening around the fireplace, speaking openly of subjects forbidden for security reasons.

Thus I learnt that Nadia was a member of the Resistance Group in the Lodz area of Poland. She had come to London to request greater help from the Polish Government in exile and was impatiently awaiting an answer, which she could not get. Her delicate oval face, very white skin, and eyes with a faraway look, contrasted sharply with the grim, vibrant determination she showed when talking. Whenever she spoke of what had happened her features hardened and her lips thinned with a cruelty in total opposition to the gentleness of her gestures. She chain-smoked while describing the blood-curdling atrocities committed by the invaders of her country. She hated everything German, but just as much, if not more, all that was Russian.

She had witnessed the meeting of the two armies, formerly allied and now at war. She had lived through her country's agony, she had been raped by both Germans and Russians.

Consigned to become a prostitute for soldiers drunk with victory, she had been thrown into a camp for a few months. She told us how she had forced herself — day after day, night after night — to hate so as to exacerbate her thirst for revenge. At a propitious moment she had slit the throat of her lover of that night in order to escape, and ever since she had kept within reach the broad-bladed knife she had used.

She could not stop talking. She felt the need to convince us of her country's sufferings, fearing that it might be victimised again at the end of the war that had inflicted such appalling agony. She realised that in London, Moscow and elsewhere a game beyond her understanding was being played for stakes which were vastly different from those for which her comrades — the Polish guerilla fighters — were dying.

Josiane, mother of a few months old baby, listened avidly, spellbound. The more blood-curdling the tales, the more details she demanded. I would have preferred not to hear.

'What kind of a woman are you to gloat over such horrors?' I asked one evening.

'I am a Gorgon', she answered, with a strange gleam in her eyes. 'I turn into stone and kill all those I love. I had a husband, he was killed in the war, I had a cat I cared for, a neighbour poisoned her. I am a channel for the forces of evil.'

Voluptuously she stretched out on the goatskin in front of the fireplace.

A medium-sized man, with delicate features and silky blond hair, overheard these words as he quietly entered the room. Rather taken aback, he apologised briefly, impressed by Josiane's fancy. Pacing up and down the room restlessly, he stopped and in a sudden outburst shouted:

'Well, love me and kill me!'

This vehement remark sounded like a shriek of anguish and silenced us. At that moment, our landlady bustled in.

'I'm not going to introduce my friend, you all know his face, famous in so many films. He has just suffered a cruel loss — Margaret, his companion, died some time ago. He is here tonight to tell us more about her and his deep sorrow.'

In the shadowy light of the room, we had indeed not recognised our visitor, although his last film, *Pygmalion,* had aroused world-wide enthusiasm just before the war.

Leaning against the mantel-piece, Leslie Howard seemed overwhelmed by grief.

'If I could only hear her voice once again', he murmured. 'Just once!'

Josiane came up to him with a gentle caressing gesture, placing her head on his shoulder. Our landlady coughed nervously.

'We could question the spirits', she suggested. 'Maybe Margaret is trying to reveal herself. Maybe she will know from beyond the grave how to give you some sign of recognition.'

'Would it be possible?' he exclaimed. 'Oh God! Would it really be possible?'

By way of reply, she brought forward a table and invited us

103

to sit round it. They started. I was just an onlooker. Under the soft lights the hands of the others joined over the pedestal table.

'Spirit, are you here', questioned our landlady. 'Reply by one jerk for yes, and two for no.'

I was watching carefully and must confess I was unable to detect any trickery. And yet. .

This first session was followed by others. I did not attend the last ones, as I had meanwhile left England. I was informed much later that Margaret's spirit manifested itself regularly. At first timidly, later more boldly. She asked her lover to present her belongings and jewels as a gift to Josiane. She also advised him to marry her. The lonely, trusting, grief-stricken lover obeyed. I don't know whether the marriage was a happy one. Anyhow, it didn't last long. Leslie Howard flew to Lisbon to take part in a tour for the troops, and the sea-plane he travelled on was lost at sea and never found.

According to documents discovered subsequently in Germany, mysterious spies had informed the Germans that Churchill was taking the Sunderland on which Howard was flying en route for Portugal.

'I am a Gorgon', Josiane had said. 'I kill those I love.'

I never saw Josiane or Nadia again. Nadia left England shortly after I did, and I was told she died fighting. I cannot recall her without sadness. The war had made her a living Errinye, one of those unforgiving goddesses of mythology. An unforgiving goddess, but — I am certain — her heart remained pure in spite of the burning hatred that devoured her.

In this story, I would have liked to omit certain events that tarnish the image of those men and women who arose to oppose tyranny and oppression.

The Resistance movement had its heroes and martyrs, but also its traitors. The verdict of history may be less clear-cut.

As few are able to perceive life's transcendent design, what appears justified at a given moment may be thought to be utterly wrong under changed circumstances.

The case I refer to is known because, after the Liberation,

the woman leader of an annihilated clandestine network accused Colonel Alric of being personally responsible for the massacre of a large number of members caught, due to his treachery.

He vehemently denied the charges, and justice did not solve the riddle. May he rest in peace. He died of a particularly painful illness a few years after his trial.

I shall recall only the facts that concerned me personally, and for simplicity's sake I shall repeat the story he told me before he was jailed and tried. The German armies were not yet beaten, but had left France.

We met in his apartment in a fashionable Paris district, his mistress, himself and I. He spoke simply.

'Do you remember', he asked me, 'that I sent London the wireless message agreed upon, namely: 'The carrots are cooked', which meant that I would be waiting for you on the date you would indicate at Cape Aiguillon, the place chosen for your return? You had agreed to give me that date as I was particularly interested in the answer you would be bringing back about the report I had entrusted you with.

'As an additional precaution, I thought it wise to send a Poste Restante card to Cannes addressed to Henri Jonquière, fixing an appointment in Marseille in case of a hitch in our plans or a last-minute change of itinerary. However, before mailing this card, the Gestapo burst into my apartment, seized it and arrested Germaine and me. Then they locked us up in a prison in Frèsnes.

'Germaine tried to commit suicide by stabbing herself in the stomach with a nail file she had hidden in the hem of her dress. She was saved by a blood transfusion: as the donor was a German nurse, she flatly refused it, screaming that she preferred to die rather than have German blood in her veins. Nevertheless, the transfusion took place.

'As for me, in order to get us out of this tight corner, I acted a part that finally paid off. I stressed my anti-Communist feelings and said I wished to have the opportunity to work with the Gestapo.

105

'They believed I was a turn-coat and quickly freed us both. But we gave them the slip and fled to Spain. After a long delay, we reached Algiers. During our journey, and in Algiers, I warned all those I considered to be in danger.'

After listening carefully to his story, I asked a single question.

'Why did you reveal not only Henri Jonquière's name, which was written on the card you could not hide, but also my real name, my addresses in Paris, and in the Free Zone, as well as that of at least one of my friends?'

'I had no choice', he answered. 'I knew you were not in France. I expected to be released before your return, a hope that unfortunately proved wrong. I also knew your friend was almost on his way out, therefore probably out of reach. In order to warn you, I had to get out of Frèsnes quickly so as to send word to change your plans. To be released I had to give tangible proof of my good faith. That is what I did, and, as you must agree, I was right, since you are alive today.'

I looked at him and shook my head. 'I owe my life to circumstances beyond your control', I said. 'I have since found out that the Germans were actually waiting for me at Cape Aiguillon on the exact date I was due to return. Only a providential delay, due to the crashing of my plane, saved me, not you!'

I have hesitated for many years before giving these facts, for my message is intended to be one of appeasement and not to arouse dormant passions.

I was asked to testify at Alric's trial as a witness for the prosecution. I had shared the agony and torment of those who had risked their lives. I do not know, even now, if I would have been able to withstand physical or mental torture. Alric loved Germaine and wanted to save her, and this may have been the reason.

Furthermore, I believe firmly that the past must be forgotten, in order to break once and for all the vicious circle hanging like a curse over men's destinies, forcing them to use repression and counter-repression without end.

Society must protect itself, but the criteria for its protection are constantly changing. As far as I am concerned, I prefer to let a higher justice run its course. 'The mills of God grind slowly, but they grind exceedingly small.' In the end, justice is done.

Let me now switch to London where I was now preparing my return to France, obviously unaware of Colonel Alric's misadventures, but having received the message: 'The carrots are cooked.'

Dereck had asked me to lunch at his club to give me final instructions.

'Be on your guard more than ever', he advised. 'The overall view has become very complicated: the German occupation of the South Zone, the Allied landing in Africa, the political split in the French camp, all this will hamper your job.'

He went on, 'I had even considered cancelling your departure. Cape Aiguillon may no longer be safe. At the moment the enemy seems to be short of sufficient forces effectively to control the Mediterranean coast. So I have kept to the original plan; now we must try to develop the route across the Pyrenees. You told me about Jaca. We'll contact Garcia. There is no problem about crossing Spain. That has been organised. See Tristan at Tarbes. He has been underground since the very beginning and will prove a great help. I am also giving you an assistant: Vivien, a young Breton. He is a first-rate wireless operator who learnt his job on a very sophisticated transmitter which he's taking with him. Everything will go, I'm sure, according to plan.'

I listened with growing uneasiness. I don't know from where it arose. Was it a normal reaction at being faced with the unknown or an indefinable premonition?

I told Dereck what I felt, since I knew he would understand.

He did not smile. Instead he said, half-seriously, half-ironically:

'Indefinable for me are the cooked carrots. Let's hope they

are cooked the way we like 'em. Why did you want Alric to meet you on landing?'

I shrugged my shoulders.

'We are on friendly terms; besides, he is also brave and efficient.'

Dereck nodded.

'Certainly, but apparently very ambitious, which explains why some people do not like him, either in London or in France. Did Carlton Gardens give you an answer to his report?'

'No', I confessed, 'unless a dilatory one can be considered negative.'

Dereck seemed lost in thought. He changed the subject and our lunch ended.

'Don't forget a London underground ticket in your pocket', he recommended jokingly. 'I'll accompany you tomorrow to the naval base where you'll be leaving from.'

After visiting my children for the last time, I was ready, almost detached from the London atmosphere. Like a stamp unstuck from an envelope, I no longer belonged to the world around me. But my forebodings were increasing.

That night I went to bed early. I slept badly, and woke up in a sweat after dreaming that I was rushing to my death under dreadful conditions. I analyzed my dream and tried to calm down.

'Why not attempt to renew the Marseille experiment? Lie outstretched, muscles relaxed', I told myself. 'Let the terrifying images unwind like a film until they stop. Place your conscious self above you. Contemplate your own fear.'

I tried in vain. My heart was pounding, and through an hitherto unknown faculty, I sensed danger.

The hours crawled by until the moment of departure. Dereck accompanied me to the naval base. Vivien was waiting for us there, eager to taste adventure. His excitement was heartening and made me forget my apprehensions.

They proved, alas, to be justified.

13

About midnight we climbed into the Sunderland.

An R.A.F. officer and an Air Marshal joined us before take-off. They were on a mission to Gibraltar where we were to meet the submarine that was taking us to France.

We took off. I tried to keep my mind a blank, but my apprehension had changed into an obsession. I was rushing to my doom.

The night was well advanced when the interphone began to crackle. The plane had been vibrating in an unusual way but, lost in thought, I had not noticed it.

A husky voice announced:

'Prepare for crash landing!'

'Meaning what?' asked Vivien, who did not understand English.

'We are dropping down!' I explained, suddenly joyful, yes joyful.

Our two travelling companions did not wait to be told twice. Unhesitatingly, they put on their Mae Wests and — as we had been ordered — joined the crew in the cockpit.

Vivien was watching me intently, totally bewildered by my unconcern.

The almost unbearable tension of the last hours broke. An extraordinary relief freed me from fear. Incredibly, I dozed off in my seat.

'Are you crazy?' the second wireless operator shouted a few minutes later. 'Put on your Mae West and follow me, for God's sake!'

The sight of Vivien, deadly pale, his teeth chattering, brought me back to reality. I quickly dragged him along to the cockpit.

Ti ti ti--Ta ta ta--Ti ti ti crackled the SOS signal. With apparent calm, the pilot announced: Altitude Zero.

He braced himself with all his strength, hauling back the joy-stick to keep the tilting plane on an even keel.

Two of the four engines had failed, one after the other. The seaplane was swaying from side to side, vibrating alarmingly. An attempt to ditch was the only solution.

'Cut off the fuel!' ordered the pilot. 'Down we go! Merry Christmas!' It was indeed Christmas Eve.

Crammed into the cockpit, we held our breaths. The plane was still flying. The sudden silence following the roar of the engines seemed rather encouraging.

We were above the Atlantic off Portugal, in order to avoid the air space of hostile Spain and neutral Portugal. Our pilot had taken a westward course; under our wings was the invisible ocean, with its tossing waves.

The engines from white hot turned to dark red. Fractions of seconds seemed like centuries. We were dropping faster and faster and a sinister whining noise was increasing.

'One, two, three, four,' counted the pilot.

At eleven, we hit the sea for the first time. Strangely enough, I did not realise the danger. To me the crash landing was providential. Was it not delivering me from an almost too vivid premonition?

We bounced like a ping-pong ball, once, twice, three times. By a miracle, we did not capsize. With the squeaking of wrenched metal sheets, the Sunderland came to a stop, still afloat. For just one minute. 'Jump!' yelled the pilot, 'Jump for your life!' We jumped through a yawning gap. The pilot threw a pneumatic raft onto the water and followed as the last to leave the wrecked aircraft.

'Pull!' I yelled to Vivien, whose hand I was holding while we both jumped into the water. To pull the cord releasing the compressed air inflating the Mae West and to pull it in at the last second on reaching the water was essential. All went well. Our life vests fully inflated, we saw the dim lights of the raft gleaming quite near. The heavy swell did not prevent us from clutching the outer ropes. The plane had disappeared, swallowed up by the ocean.

'Eight out of eight', stated the pilot counting our heads. 'Now pull yourselves onto the raft, then search the pockets on each

110

side of this ocean liner. You'll find something to drink. Let us celebrate our shipwreck with dignity and enjoy our pleasure cruise.'

I could not help admiring him. He certainly had guts and a fine sense of humour. I still experienced no fear.

Drenched to the skin, we hoisted ourselves onto the raft one after the other. Whisky flasks were soon discovered and passed around. We swallowed draught after draught to the health of the King, blessing the forethought of those responsible for supplying the needs of the shipwrecked. A pleasant warmth was creeping up while we boisterously sang *It's a long way to Tipperary* and *Lili Marlene*. We were alive, lost on the boundless Atlantic. But soon euphoria gave way to bitter cold. Shivering, tossed about, we rapidly became seasick. Prostrated, I wished to die.

Dawn broke. A pale wintry sun broke through the mist covering the immense and endless ocean. The swell grew stronger, the wind was howling. We lay in the bottom of the raft more dead than alive, weakened, dejected, hopeless.

'Boat on port side!' shouted somebody. These magic words brought us to life, making us forget our misery. The instinct for survival is indomitable.

Indeed, not too far away, a large fishing boat was heading straight for us. We waved our handkerchiefs, Mae Wests, anything that was at hand. The boat was approaching fast. Undoubtedly we had been spotted.

We learned later that the *Marie Christina's* master had picked up our S.O.S. and was searching for us.

'Take off your clothes!' shouted the pilot who had recovered his energy. 'Throw them overboard! Hurry!'

We stared at him, bewildered. He explained, while he set the example. 'Whoever rescues us, whether friend or enemy, we are all servicemen, shipwrecked soldiers; civilian and military underwear are the same.'

He was one hundred per cent right. Vivien and I were travelling in civilian clothes. We undressed hastily, throwing our things into the water.

111

The boat was now very near. What was her nationality? Portuguese, Spanish or.... German?

Our minds were soon set at rest. A feverish agitation was reigning on the bridge. Orders, counter-orders, were being issued in Portuguese. Luck was on our side.

Those good sailors, little experienced in life-saving procedures, eager to help, almost rammed us. They were bustling about and getting in each other's way. An accident was avoided in the nick of time. We were soon hoisted on board, wrapped in blankets and enjoying the invigorating warmth of mugfuls of toddy.

As I had a smattering of Spanish, I was elected interpreter. Although the two Hispanic languages have a common root, they are actually quite different. I guessed rather than understood the *Maria Christina*'s master when he came to enquire about our comfort but also to satisfy his curiosity.

'Why the hell did you undress on the raft?' he asked.

At a loss, I gazed questioningly at the pilot who was lying at his ease on a blanket.

'Tell him that we are doing our physical training', he suggested, without smiling.' One does it in underpants, why make a fuss about it.'

I gestured the answer as well as I could. It took some time before the captain understood, and when he did, he spat on the floor to show his dismay.

'It's quite impossible,' he cried, 'for a God-fearing man to understand the English! They're mad. Physical training on a raft at the mercy of the waves! Did one ever hear of anything crazier!'

Spluttering indignantly he left, while we choked with laughter.

That afternoon, we reached Leixos.

The Portuguese authorities were waiting for us when we berthed. They interrogated us in the harbour premises, but more as a matter of form.

According to prior agreement, we said we were British servicemen on our way to Gibraltar.

112

Vivien was asked how it was possible that a British serviceman could not speak English. We had foreseen the question and Vivien was able to reply promptly:

'I am a national of Mauritius Island, where we speak only French, although it's His Majesty's dominion.'

The interrogator was quite satisfied as he was indeed ready to accept any story.

When the questioning was over, we were allowed to see the British Consul who had come upon hearing the news, and even to talk to him alone.

'I've brought you dry underwear and clothes, toothbrushes and soap; you'll need them in prison.'

'In prison?'

'Quite so', he smiled. 'For the duration.' He paused significantly. 'Unless you escape before.'

'And how does one escape from Portuguese gaols?' we enquired, getting the hint.

'With my help and the full sympathy of the local authorities!' he assured us, and burst out laughing. 'Don't you know that the only international treaty — four centuries old — that has never been annulled is the one between England and Portugal. You're lucky devils. Franco would not have welcomed you so well. You'll see. You'll escape in due course.'

'When? Where? How?'

'You'll learn soon enough. Until then, patience. Tonight I've ordered you some roast chicken. It will be served to you in prison. Good luck, have a good time. Now I must go.'

We climbed into a mini-bus and under a proper escort we entered the gaol to Oporto.

Before going to our respective cells we were served a hearty meal in the rest room. The roast chicken held a prominent position on the menu.

Heartened by the thought that our imprisonment would be of short duration, we tried to make the best of it. Being privileged, we were allowed to get together for meals delivered daily by a nearby restaurant; we could also play cards and chess and read at will.

I shared a cell with a convict, condemned for having helped his two wives to reach a better world.

'I could have avoided being caught', he admitted ruefully, 'had I not made the mistake of using the same method twice. But it worked so beautifully the first time.'

About ten days after our imprisonment, the Chief Superintendent whispered into my ear that we should have a haircut. We took the hint and followed his advice immediately. Walking along the corridor, we found an open door and a passage leading to the administration offices where the Consul was waiting. He escorted us quite openly to two cars parked on a side-street, and thus we succeeded in staging our miraculous escape.

Of the days I had spent locked in my cell, I retained the memory of an experience I have no wish to repeat. The sensation of being deprived of liberty is terrible and whenever I go to a zoo I suffer for the caged animals. Freedom is the essence of all things and to disregard it is to destroy the meaning of life.

The Consul invited me to spend a few days at his home on the outskirts of the town. 'Your comrades', he explained, 'will leave immediately for Gibraltar. From there, Vivien will return to London, since the Service has not yet decided upon your future moves.'

I accepted willingly, having taken an immediate liking to him. He was, as I found later, a most interesting and cultured man.

While showing me round his well-kept grounds, he proudly pointed out a rotunda fitted out as a library. I spent most of my days there. Wide bay-windows opened onto a dream panorama. In the distance the sea sparkled, bordered by well wooded hills. Nearby vineyards rippled over the contours of the landscape, separated by cypress trees pointing their dark pinnacles skywards.

An open fire provided pleasant warmth. Bookcases arranged in quincunx shelves were laden with tempting volumes, and reading often merged into meditation. Comfortable leather armchairs alternated with cushions piled on the floor on wild animal skins.

At the end of the third day of heavenly peace, as I was admiring the ochre tints of sunset from one of the bay windows, my host entered the room. He poured himself a drink according to a precise ritual: two cubes of ice, a few measures of whisky, and a drop of lemon squash.

Sipping his drink, absent-mindedly fondling the head of a stuffed tiger, he bluntly announced:

'You are flying to London tomorrow. From Lisbon.'

Expecting this decision, I started to thank him for his hospitality, but he stopped me with a gesture:

'Your guardian angel was certainly wide awake. Had the plane not crashed you would have been heading into disaster. It seems certain that the enemy had arranged for a reception committee at Cape Aiguillon.'

He waved aside the questions I was anxious to ask before he even finished the sentence.

'I know nothing more. Such matters are beyond my competence. Let's have dinner. London alone knows the answers.'

We talked late into the night. We discussed the reasons for war and deplored man's lack of wisdom. We philosophised and our thoughts met on more than one point.

'Do you believe in the supernatural?' asked my host, switching suddenly to another subject.

His question caused me to ponder. I had never put it to myself directly, and I dimly felt that by giving an honest answer I would have to pass beyond a barrier my logical mind had erected against the dangers of my winged imagination. The moment of truth had arrived unexpectedly. Would I dare cast aside my crutches, and dash towards...towards what?

I hesitated, as I gazed at the flames dancing in the fire-place. Would I burn my bridges?

My host, guessing my inner conflict, kept silent.

I shall always remember that, suddenly, something within me let go. I left the shelter, I forgot the ground beneath my feet to enter another dimension. I emerged into the unknown, forsaking all that until then had seemed safe and solid.

I passed over a threshold towards an unknown and hidden

world I wished to explore. I have not turned back since.

The next day the Consul, who had become my friend, took me to the station. When the train to Lisbon started with a jerk, he stood to attention and, in a low voice, sang the first few notes of the *Marseillaise*. It was his way of wishing me luck.

A few hours later I arrived in Lisbon.

I walked to the address I had been given. A young woman greeted me. She regarded me closely before leading the way to the office of a burly middle-aged man. We shook hands and turning to her, he asked smilingly:

'Did you imagine that your beloved looked just like him?'

Smiling at my astonishment, he introduced his secretary.

'This is Rhea. It was to her you addressed your passionate love-letters from Marseille.'

Rhea blushed. So did I.

'Did you read my messages?'

'Of course', she answered, 'Do you know a woman who doesn't read love-letters? Unfortunately the Service quickly took them away. What a pity your declarations of eternal faith were just faked. I could have imagined they were sincere!' With a sigh of mock despair, she withdrew.

I saw her again before leaving Lisbon. On duty, she escorted me to the airport.

'Send me a postcard from London, but this time do write to me and to me only. Goodbye! Good luck and God bless you!'

I promised I would.

So once again I landed in an airport near the British capital. But I was not the same man who had left three weeks earlier.

The lucky course of events had made me aware that one's destiny is interwoven with hundreds of threads criss-crossing in many ways, making it impossible to guess the final design.

This I could not do. I was impatient to respond to what I felt was written in my destiny, anxious to return to France as soon as possible.

In London, I learnt from the Service that Alric had been

arrested by the Gestapo and the Villa Isabelle searched from top to bottom.

'You are blown, old chap', concluded Dereck. 'To return is out of the question.'

I protested vigorously.

'I have no intention of rotting in England. The Line has not been affected. Drop me over in France. I'll keep away from the places where Frédéric Lionel is known. Henri Jonquière can be safely forgotten. The Pyrenees will be the centre of operations and I'll settle with Tristan in Tarbes, since you have spoken so highly of him and his friends.'

He took a lot of convincing. Finally, he surrendered, and agreed to send me to a Commando School for parachute training as — according to regulations — five drops were required before one was considered ready to land on enemy territory.

I accepted, happy that a solution had been found. I reminded him of his words: 'Each of us must be determined to assume his destiny.'

He could only nod his agreement.

14

A squat, slate-roofed grey building at the foot of a green hill, a heather-carpeted moor shrouded in steamy mist which blurred the crest of the nearby mountain: that was how the Commando School appeared to me on the first day I reported for duty.

The mist seldom lifted. When it did, the sea could be seen at some distance, moving in a constant swell. Far away — weather permitting — one could imagine the wave-beaten Shetland Isles.

If the sun broke through the heavy clouds looming over the Northern-most tip of Scotland, the area conveyed an impression of melancholy mixed with some charm.

Totally isolated, near the dormant waters of two lakes, the school was eminently suitable for training thirty recruits.

On the deserted moor we were taught how to kill and how to avoid being killed. It was a tough training. The day started at four-thirty a.m. with a cup of tea, followed — regardless of the weather — by one hour of physical drill that meant marching and climbing at the double. Paradoxical though it may seem, we felt an acute pleasure in pushing ourselves beyond our physical limit.

Some of us were trained as saboteurs, but all were taught how to handle explosives. We used dynamite and plastics with a total lack of concern. We organised glorious fireworks, blowing up life-sized models, using incredible amounts of explosives.

We learnt to use every kind of weapon to find our bearings on moonless nights, to dodge blows, to use any tool available, to escape through the air ducts or narrow drains in order to save our lives; we were taught to be on the alert without showing it, and how to avoid reactions so as to assess risks calmly without interference from instinctive impulses.

In short, we were turned into relentless fighters prepared to show no mercy to anyone. Fortunately, I never had to apply these techniques.

I fought the enemy without killing anybody — on the contrary, by saving people in danger. But I am aware all the same that the self-mastery acquired brought success to impossible operations and strengthened my confidence in my own powers.

Final tests before leaving the school called for courage, quick thinking and initiative. They included the crossing of a road swept by real machine-gun fire, hooked to a rope suspended on to a branch; jumping into a deep gully, swimming in a river against strong currents; running faster than trained dogs; taking over a locomotive, breaking through a road-block and other similar feats.

Towards the end, I felt physically and morally ready for anything.

From the Commando School I was sent to the parachute

school. I enjoyed my first jump which gave me the impression of being released from gravity. Finally, came the long-awaited moment of my return to France.

We were skimmimg the ground, which did not prevent the anti-aircraft guns from firing occasionally. The night was peaceful. The moon was full. The blinker turned green: 'Go', yelled the lieutenant, after checking my parachute straps. I was off.

Sucked earthwards, I dropped. A cow lowed. The familiar sound relaxed my taut nerves. I landed normally, rolling over, happy to touch the soil of France. I was home again.

Mechanically I went through the prescribed motions. I buried my parachute, and with the aid of a luminous compass found my bearings and strode along the road leading to a nearby station. I was scheduled to take a train to Toulouse in the early morning and from there onto Tarbes.

The time has come to tell of some heroic, comic and dramatic events which made up the stirring history of this unusual period.

I dedicate these lines to my living and dead companions. Very inadequately I have tried to describe their loyalties and self-sacrifices. They reveal a sacred union formed by men fighting side by side, stimulated by a hope which can be summed up by the last words of General de Gaulle's appeal of June 18, 1940:

'Our country is in deadly danger. Let us fight to save it!'

It was on hearing these words in the dining-room of a small inn, more bistro than restaurant, in Tarbes, that a few men formed the first resistance network in Bigorre, a county bordered by the Pyrenees. Tristan, the inn-keeper, embodies the type of French shadow fighter of whom little is said because he had no political ties, no ideological affiliations, and no self-centred aims.

Bent by rheumatism, unable to turn his head from one side to the other, walking with the aid of two sticks, reckless and

119

oblivious to danger, his authority and determination always found a solution to impossible problems. Food, clothing and lodging for parcels in transit were just a few of them. Tristan's bistro became the despatch centre and almost the Line's HQ. We learnt later that it was listed as a terrorist lair both by the French Militia, collaborating with the Germans, and the occupying forces.

With the support of his wife and two daughters, he never spared himself, always ready to help friends involved in underground activities. I saw him smiling derisively during dramatic incidents.

I remember a search carried out by Georgians of the Vlassov Army, a Russian general who embraced the German cause. They burst upon us one day at noon, lined us up against a wall, our hands crossed above our heads. They searched the house from top to bottom, ripping everything open with their bayonets. That day, in one of the ground-floor closets was a suitcase crammed full with automatics, grenades and explosives brought in the night before by a member of a sabotage group.

The vandals smashed their way through everything, while Tristan kept protesting against the outrage. His wife and daughters joined loudly in the chorus of protest.

Their attitude was so different from what one might expect from guilty people that the detachment's commanding officer stopped the search at the very moment when one of his men opened the door of the closet. The suitcase was well in view, but the soldiers did not rip it up, and maybe because my guardian angel was wide awake, neglected to open it.

The Georgians left, threatening to be back soon, leaving us all in a cold sweat.

I remember an implacable Tristan making fun of my weakness when he had asked me to accompany him to a trailer parked on the sports-ground of the city, in the very centre of the town.

Youths from a nearby maquis had imprisoned a militiaman in one of the trailers. They had tortured him to extract information about one of their comrades who had been arrested. More dead than alive, the militiaman had promised to tell what he knew to an officer of the regular forces.

Tristan took me to the spot. On entering the trailer, the stench of scorched flesh, blood, and vomit filled my nostrils. I nearly fainted at the sight of the living corpse lying at my feet.

Not a gleam of pity could be detected in the eyes of the hate-filled torturers. The militiaman stammered a few words, prayed for God's forgiveness, and died.

I also remember Tristan when he was slapped in the face by a self-appointed Commissar in a Communist-occupied part of France (and there were many) just after the German retreat. It is true that the alleged Commissar thought that he was dealing with collaborators. Confusion was at its peak at that period. Final victory was around the corner, and the already liberated country was in a state of violent unrest. Tristan, roaring with rage, leapt forward, quite forgetting his two sticks which fell to the ground, and grabbed the throat of his aggressor. We narrowly escaped being summarily shot on the spot!

In the town of La Souterraine, or rather, in a nearby castle, I handed over a machine-gun to General Redon, Commander of the Secret Army. Nowadays, whenever we meet, he recalls this event because of its symbolic value.

Tristan recruited guides able to lead parcels to the Spanish side of the Pyrenees. It was in his inn that numerous identity cards were forged. It was his idea — thanks to an obliging head consultant of the local hospital — to hide parcels in the ward reserved for contagious patients.

One day, Gestapo agents decided to search the hospital from top to bottom. On hearing this the consultant raised his eyes to heaven in despair. 'I must point out' he told them, 'that one wing is reserved for patients with contagious diseases. The dangers of infection are great. If you insist on searching this ward then I must disclaim all responsibility!'

The Gestapo looked at each other with some apprehension. Finally, they decided against it. Behind the closed door to the ward were three parcels awaiting transportation.

I could go on quoting countless similar events, but it would mean forgetting my main objective. So I beg all those who fought side-by-side to recognise themselves in Tristan without bitterness at not having been mentioned individually.

Yet I must pay special homage to the many women who co-operated with us with unswerving courage. Let me end this chapter by telling just one story about a young girl sent by a friend in Carcassonne with an important message for London.

She hid it in her bicycle pump. After riding through most of the night, she was stopped at daybreak at a German road-block. The soldiers needed bikes, so the Feldwebel promptly requisitioned hers. Annoyed, but by no means discouraged, the girl sat on the side of the road and proposed a deal with the NCO, now owner of her bicycle.

'I'll kiss you', she promised, 'in exchange for the bicycle pump. It's a souvenir and I am fond of it.'

The girl was beautiful. The Feldwebel agreed, and the message reached London.

I hope that the reader is able to follow the progress of my slowly growing inner transformation. Preconceived ideas hampering an understanding previously based on rationality were vanishing. The intensity of the action in which I was involved favoured this transformation. Moreover, as the means of perception awakened I could begin to observe, rather than submit to the pressures of cruelty and fear existing in the microcosm of embattled Europe.

Let me try to cast some light on the process enabling me to reach consciousness of a greater Reality hitherto veiled from me by a world consumed by passions and inhumanity.

Only serenity makes it possible to act so as to remain an unbiased spectator of the world as it is, to make the correct choice freely and assume one's responsibilities.

However, before winding up the first part of this account of events ending with the Liberation of Paris, I need to mention two important facts — just two of the many incidents which made the Line what it was. The first was the arrival of Captain

Jacques in France; the second, my unforeseen trip to Spain.

I was moving around constantly towards the end of the war in order to keep in touch with the safe-houses and the escort of parcels. Always there was the risk of being recognised by those who had my photograph on record, ever since their failure to capture me at Cape Aiguillon.

Under the name of Fernand Lambert, I had rented a flat in Paris, near the Mirabeau bridge. I cycled quite confidently along the streets of the city, avoiding the places where Frédéric Lionel was known, in particular around my apartment where a police-trap had been set. One day I passed in front of the house and felt the looming danger behind the deceptive calm of the exterior. The trap I was supposed to fall into had been kept open for the duration. That is why none of my belongings were touched, in Paris or in Amphion.

Those on the look-out refrained from searching my apartment, hoping against hope to see me caught.

It was at this time that the Service, in order to strengthen transmission facilities before D-Day, despatched to France, Captain Jacques, a top radio operator known for his calmness.

Jacques was dropped by parachute at about four a.m. onto a site we had marked. It was the morning of a day which became memorable for two reasons. First, by the quick succession of unexpected events, and second, because some of them took on a particular importance, entailing deeds not inspired by logical reasoning but by intuition, backed by an innermost belief in something beyond logic.

Maurice, one of Tristan's comrades, expected Jacques on a lonely plateau fifty miles outside Tarbes. We had borrowed from our guests (which is what we mockingly called the Germans), a Citröen car with German Army markings.

Jacques' jump went off smoothly. The well worked-out routine for this kind of operation was performed in record time. Quickly we settled in the car: Maurice at the steering wheel, I beside him, and Jacques on the back seat, two transmitters camouflaged in a couple of worn leather suitcases at his feet.

On a country road we almost ran into a fallen tree on a bend.

It happened at the edge of a wood. We stopped, and were immediately surrounded by maquis fighters, waving their weapons and forcing us to drive into the wood.

Mistaken for Germans, we were dragged from the car, searched and compelled to empty our pockets, those around us shouting 'Death to the traitors'. We quickly realised that they wanted to shoot us on the spot, believing that we were, if not Germans, at least members of the hated militia.

Their chief — a youngster of about twenty — examined my two identity cards, one French and the other German. Having borrowed a German vehicle, I had taken appropriate identity papers, but had kept the French ones in case of need. The youngster came to the conclusion that we were highly dangerous individuals.

'They are skunks', he shouted. 'Blindfold them and rid the world of these rats.'

I went on parleying as persuasively as I could:

'Look at our transmitters. Look at the English code in the suitcase, cross-examine Jacques who was in London yesterday. Don't make a bloody fool of yourself!'

Finally, thank God, the intensity of my pleading shook the determination of these very young and inexperienced fighters who had only recently joined the maquis.

'Death to the traitors!' yelled a Czech, brandishing a sharpened kitchen knife under my nose. Feeling his companion's hesitation, he was obviously prepared to act as executioner himself.

I confess that the knife frightened me more than the incongruous medley of weapons held by the youngsters who had taken us prisoner.

Finally, after long palavers, they grasped the true facts. But the sun was high in the sky when we finally left the inhospitable spot after recovering our property and receiving a crate of fruit as a gift.

Maurice put the crate on a rack on the roof of the car.

'What next?' he asked. 'Do we wait here until nightfall?'

'We'd better take the risk of driving home rather than

sticking around,' I said. 'They may still change their minds.'

So we drove on, but not for long. Another road-block down a lane brought us to an abrupt halt. About fifty Wehrmacht soldiers pointed their guns at us.

'Raus!' roared their captain. 'Get out!'

We complied, Maurice and Jacques with their hands above their heads, while I, seemingly unconcerned, climbed out calmly.

I was, and I realised it only later, quite outside myself. I let go, my mind a blank. I was free from fear.

Walking towards the Captain, I asked him in German the reason for stopping us.

'Papers!' he ordered sharply.

At this critical moment, my behaviour was completely illogical. I deliberately handed him my French identity card.

'You are French?' he asked increduously, gazing at my papers and at the W.H. on the car, meaning Wehrmacht-Heer.

I nodded, gazing at him steadily.

'As I hold French papers, you must accept that I am French.'

Speaking perfect German, I stressed the word must. A gleam of understanding flickered in his eyes. Obviously, he guessed I was a Gestapo agent, pretending to be a Frenchman. I saw by his expression how his mind was working. I took the crate off the rack and offered fruit all round.

Turning to Maurice, I said:

'Lower your hands, we are among friends.'

Jacques fortunately grasped the situation, although totally ignorant of Goethe's language. In spite of his nonchalance, sweat trickled down his trousers. The tension had been paralysing for someone in the field for the first time.

Nobody noticed it, except perhaps the Feldwebel who grabbed one of the two suitcases concealing the transmitters. I barely had time to ask the Captain.

'You are having our things searched?'

'Of course not', he said, turning to the suspicious N.C.O. 'In Ordnung!' Drop it.

The N.C.O. shook his head. 'I'm only doing my duty.'

The two locks clicked, releasing the lid. The wings of Death grazed us. The end was close, very, very close.

'*Disziplin schwach!*' — poor discipline, I said loudly, in that fraction of a second preceding disclosure. That a Gestapo agent should criticise the discipline in a Wehrmacht unit required an immediate denial.

'Put those suitcases back instantly!' roared the Captain. 'Step on it.'

The locks clicked again, closing the lid. Sullenly, the Feldwebel replaced the two transmitters.

No words can describe my feelings.

I took leave casually, thanking the Captain for his courtesy. Maurice took the steering wheel. Jacques and I resumed our seats.

Just before driving off, the Captain bent forward and warned me that he had ordered a second road-block to be set up about twenty miles further on.

'There are terrorists everywhere,' he explained. 'Take care, my friend, for they are trigger happy. To pass through give the password: Captain Krause, my name. My apologies for the delay. Heil Hitler!'

Maurice let in the clutch and drove off at top speed.

'Christ! You've certainly got guts' he exclaimed. But he was wrong. It was nothing to do with guts, but an intangible, powerful something that I cannot explain.

We passed the second road-block without a hitch. But as the proverb rightly says: 'All things go in threes.'

In the vicinity of Rabastens and very near to my HQ, we were again stopped by the maquis. This time we were so worn out that we did not even defend ourselves.

Surrounded by a yelling group of frenzied boys, we were compelled to drive the Citröen into a barn. One of them went to fetch Tristan, confident that, by handing over an exceptional catch to Major Edward, whom he had heard was Tristan's friend, he would be awarded the V.C.

The youngsters were not aware that Major Edward and I were one and the same person. They knew of my existence by hearsay, and so — thank God — Tristan arrived. He understood, he laughed, and teased those who wanted to hand me over to myself.

It really was a memorable day!

15

Urgent reasons called me to Spain, though I had no wish to stay longer than twenty-four hours. At my suggestion, the Service arranged a meeting between Garcia and myself and an emissary I asked them to send, in a charcoal burners' hut not far from the French frontier.

I attached great importance to this meeting because Jean, the son of my friend Paul in Marseille, had suddenly shown up in Tarbes two weeks earlier. He wished to join the French Forces in England.

I was particularly anxious to avoid any hitches and make his passage as easy as possible. I had asked Vasco, one of our most reliable guides — he had been an officer in the Spanish Republican Army — to act as escort across the border and hand him over to Garcia; he would then be channelled through the links leading to Gibraltar.

Vasco and Jean failed to reach Garcia. We learned that they had been arrested. Vasco had been unable to resist the temptation of seeing his wife whom he had left behind years before. To be nearer to him, she had managed to move into the vicinity of the Trans-Pyrenean escape route she knew he used, misjudging the close watch kept upon her.

I had decided to use my authority to impress upon the emissary the importance I attached to the efforts the Service should make in obtaining Jean's release from the Miranda camp. I knew that the Spanish Government was far more flexible than previously. Vasco, who was imprisoned at Figueras and in danger of being executed, must also receive whatever help was possible.

Always resourceful, Garcia would, I hoped, find ways and means nobody had thought of. Moreover, I was looking forward to meeting him again.

Having chosen a professional mountain guide to lead me over the border we started at Sainte-Marie-de-Campans, a small village high up in the Pyrenees. To reach there I cycled at night since the whole area was a prohibited zone and the 'Alpenjäger' — the German Alpine Corps — were swarming everywhere.

We left the village at dawn. Our track ran through moraines and glaciers, up and down gorges, as we climbed to snowy peaks. The going was very hard. I blessed my training in Scotland, but nevertheless found it difficult to keep up with my guide for eighteen hours at a stretch.

Too tired to eat any solid food, I drank milk whenever we found any of the camouflaged hiding places prepared by the shepherds.

Suddenly, near a boundary-stone on a mountain crest, we came upon an exhausted, more than half-starved couple. The two young people had attempted the mountain crossing without assistance or sufficient food. Weakened by fatigue and hunger, unable to continue, frozen and shivering, they had sheltered under a rock to await death. When we found them, they had given up hope. We managed to light a small brush-wood fire and after a few gulps of brandy they took heart again. We left them our provisions while I told them how best to act.

'Spain is just over the crest. Climb down into the valley on any path you can find. Eat and get back your strength. Forget our meeting completely. Give yourselves up to the first frontier-guard you meet. Sorry I can't give you any other advice. Spain has become more lenient towards refugees and you won't be interned for long.'

Sitting round a blackened iron pot hanging from a trivet over a charcoal fire, the smoke struggling to escape through an opening in the roof, we exchanged our impressions.

Lindsay, the Service emissary posted to Madrid, promised to take every possible step to get Jean out of the Miranda camp. 'Maybe within a month' he said. And he actually succeeded. The Vasco problem was, however, beyond his control, and he saw little hope.

Garcia was less pessimistic.

'I might be able to get the help of a friend', he suggested, 'a high-up in the prison admin in Barcelona. I'll let you know.'

The help worked, but we only learnt this eleven years later.

Vasco escaped and returned to France. He told an incredible story. Sometime after our meeting, an order for his release did in fact arrive at the Figueras prison. Unfortunately, on the day of his release a general had chosen to inspect the prison. He questioned the validity of an order supposedly issued by his own service and the man who signed it got into serious trouble. To kiss his wife just once had cost Vasco eleven years of freedom.

That evening round the fire, isolated from the world in a huge forest, we felt very distant from the war.

The smoke got into our eyes; the occasional crackling of a branch catching fire underlined our reveries.

'Garcia, tell us more about Alchemy!'

I heard myself uttering these words as if somebody else had spoken them. They reflected a not yet fully conscious longing, daily growing stronger.

I was not thinking of Alchemy as one imagines it, maybe as it was experienced by the so-called 'blowers' in the Middle Ages, men interested only in physical results. I saw it as a science of the mysteries of nature, of hidden forces offering an answer to my quest for the reasons which had plunged so many people into suffering and death.

The glowing embers lit up our faces. I closed my eyes waiting for a reply, wishing to concentrate in order not to miss a word.

A few minutes elapsed.

'Alchemy', began Garcia, 'is the science of invisible and dynamic energies. These energies are the ones bringing cohesion to the molecule, the ones bringing life to our bodies.

They pulsate in the cosmos and are of such subtle nature that they cannot be observed. The appearance of things conceals what appears not. One may ask 'What does appear not? Can it be understood?' The Alchemist answers 'Yes'. His assertion is supported by a mythical and mystical legacy which enjoins him to seek the truth in the depths of our inner-being, as any atom in the body takes part in the cosmic movement, manifesting Life and revealing its Law.

'Know thyself and thou shalt know the Universe and its Gods. This is the motto of the true Alchemist.

'To know the Law of Life, uniting in true fraternity the mineral, the vegetable, and the human worlds, enables the adept who understands, to reign over Matter by Spirit. Cognition on this level is revealed by the esoteric symbolism of numbers, a philosophy which constitutes the link between Universal Intelligence and its manifestation in the tangible world. The Cosmic rhythm with the innumerable interactions of pulsating energies can be expressed by numbers, not mathematical but archetypal symbols.'

He stopped. The silence was complete. There were so many questions I would have liked to ask. But dawn was breaking, the sky was turning pink. We rose.

Lindsay left us reluctantly, while Garcia, full of energy, in spite of a sleepless night, said:

'I'll join you. I love mountaineering and to return to Jaca the long way round will be delightful.'

I was only too glad. After a light breakfast, we set off.

My feet were painful and fatigue, until then forgotten, became overwhelming.

Climbing was arduous. I slipped constantly over the stony moraine and on the snow patches covering the polished rocks with their sharp edges.

I have always been receptive to the spell of mountains. They rise massive and powerful, yet serene and dignified, as if to reveal Eternity to mankind. The trees growing on their sides seem to transmit a sense of greatness, and the wind humming through their tops evokes an echo of the Infinite.

In the mountains, plants have brighter colours, the water is crystal-clear, and the meadows greener. Their magic grips you even after so laborious an ascent. I felt it in spite of my weariness. But enchantment suddenly gave way to fear.

'Look out!' cried Garcia, pointing downwards.

Three figures in grey-green uniforms, kneeling at the edge of a wood, were aiming their rifles at us, and their weapons, we guessed, were equipped with telescopic sights. Our guide automatically reached for the Sten gun he was carrying. Garcia stopped him.

'It's useless', he whispered, 'your toy lacks the range. Let's continue our descent as if unaware of the danger.'

Turning to me, he added:

'Be calm, let yourself be filled by a force beyond logic. Be only your higher self. Forget all fear.'

I tried to follow his advice. I tried to be the onlooker of my own behaviour, in short, to repeat the successful experiment achieved in Marseille. I do not believe I rose above the anxiety which held me in its grip, and if I did pass into a state of unconcernedness I had little time to realise it.

It is sometimes difficult to believe in miracles. Nevertheless, they occur, and I couldn't believe it. A cloud, the only one hanging like a banner to the towering peak, started to move across the mountain. Soon we were wrapped in mists.

Without hesitation, we started running as fast as we could to keep pace with the drifting cloud.

We were blotted from sight. When we finally stopped for breath, we had reached another slope with no soldiers in view. This miracle completes the first part of my story. The second part is less eventful.

The Liberation of Europe began. Wonderful, exhilarating, intoxicating, but with dramatic bloodshed, useless killings and petty revenge.

I played my part both in Tarbes and in nearby Lourdes; everything seemed to happen at once. I tried to appease hatred and the urge for vengeance, particularly strong in these regions of hot-blooded men and women.

131

I shall never forget the sight of the blazing stable, surrounded by a clamorous crowd, howling its hatred.

One of my men had hastened to fetch me. Walking back with him at the double, he told me what had happened.

'You ordered us to keep watch over the prisoners. We locked them up in the stable and put guards on the door. You know the building, it is solid and the six skylights on the upper part of the walls are fitted with iron bars. Besides, they didn't want to give us the slip, knowing all that could save them from being torn to pieces was your decision to hand them over to the regulars.'

'Come to the point' I said.

'They are all dead. Hernandez and his two crazy friends threw grenades through the skylights on the opposite side of the building.'

We ran towards the farm where the stable was situated. But the tragedy was over. The straw and hay stored inside had caught fire and the roof had collapsed.

Hernandez, who had guided us across the Pyrenees, refused to listen to my protests.

'War is slaughter' he shouted. 'The defeated must pay and the cost is high. The Geneva Convention? To hell with it! Vermin must be exterminated'.

He turned his back and left whistling under his breath. An eye for an eye and a tooth for a tooth.

Nor shall I forget the summary execution of the Gestapo chief in an Arriège village. The afternoon was drawing to its close. The imposing setting of the mountains seemed to defy the men who were preparing his execution, the *pièce de résistance* as it were, of the liberation festivities.

The inhabitants had crowded round, determined not to miss a second.

'Don't interfere', warned the local Maquis chief, with a hint of a threat in his voice. 'Whether you approve or not, the filthy swine must pay for his crimes.'

I shrugged my shoulders. No appeasement was possible. This was their moment of triumph.

Nor could I leave without losing face among my own men. I

sat down on the slope of the road and scrutinised the condemned man.

He had a soldierly bearing. Tightly buttoned in his black SS uniform, impeccable in spite of the dust staining it, a monocle in his eye, he waited impassively, ignoring the three men flanking him, their fingers on the triggers of their sten-guns.

A gun-carrier taken from the enemy, moved forward driven by a maquisard. It stopped under the horizontal branch of a plane tree.

'Death', yelled the crowd.

'Hang the swine, get on with the job! — Make him pay!'

The SS colonel stood up without waiting for orders. Followed by his guards he advanced without hesitation. He jumped on the platform of the carrier — and waited.

The Maquis chief quickly threw a rope over the branch of the tree tying it round his victim's neck. Then he stood back.

'Take it away', he shouted.

The carrier leapt forward. The show, however, was not yet over. Badly tied to the branch, the rope slipped and the colonel fell heavily to the ground, the rope's noose still round his neck.

He got up quickly, apparently unmoved. Flouting those standing by, he picked up his monocle, wiped it carefully on his jacket, adjusted it, and with an imperious snap of his fingers beckoned the driver of the carrier to move back.

Nobody stirred. Stupefied, the onlookers allowed him to direct the manoeuvre.

The carrier returned to its starting point. With a gesture of contempt he jumped onto the platform. Then, with a calculated movement he threw the free end of the rope over the branch, securing it by several turns. Finally, with a sharp tug he checked its resistance.

'Go', yelled the Maquis chief, who until then had kept silent.

'Go', repeated the colonel in English.

No shout of triumph greeted his death. Courage always inspires respect.

What lesson can be drawn from an attitude showing a total disdain of death? Indoctrination does not explain it, nor is

133

patriotism a satisfactory answer. Yet the Nazi National Socialist movement had its own terrifying mysticism.

When Paris was liberated, Jacques and I were able to board a Fieseler-Storch plane in Toulouse. Piloted by a member of the Secret Army, we flew over central France, still under German control, and landed at Le Bourget airport.

On our arrival Tristan's daughters had run up with such materials as they could lay their hands on, two so-called English uniforms, as they imagined them to be. As we passed a group of American soldiers, one of them pointed at us and said to his companion:

'Say, what in hell uniform is that?'

'Bulgarian' replied the other.

16

My outlook had changed profoundly. I now understood that if fighting is unavoidable then to fight with detachment and without hatred is an ideal prompted by chivalry and is also innate in human nature, too often distorted by passion and revengefulness.

All victories are ephemeral and revenge only breeds revenge, generating an endless vicious cycle. Yet war had broadened my vision. False concepts had been replaced by perception of an acuteness sometimes resented by others. Yet my new outlook was located in a dichotomy which filled me with utter disillusion. The behaviour of the victors at every level was far different from what I had naïvely hoped.

False decisions and their consequences set in motion a new cycle of error, little different from the pre-war world. It made me think that it is impossible to leave the beaten track —

another cause for despondency! Only years later did I fully understand the psychological revolution needed to make a real change possible. And when I finally attempted it, success was due to a woman — my second wife.

I met Geneviève by chance, that useful word which whitewashes our ignorance of the workings of fate. It happened, yet it might not have, through my own decision. The paths of destiny are revealed by a number of factors we do not understand: yet we know that our decisions can change our lives.

How did I meet her? Tristan and about twenty of our comrades came to Paris a short time after my return there, and we set out to celebrate. Von Runstedt's counter-offensive had not yet been launched. The allies were forging ahead on all fronts: victory was near. My friends and I went in jubilant mood to the Tabarin. We had dined, and were happy to be alive and together. We all felt like dancing. I had no partner and I rose to ask the nearest woman to our table. I could only see her fair hair, for she was sitting looking away from me.

We have seldom parted since. At that time, however, I had no intention of starting a new life with Geneviève. I was far too absorbed in my children's future and my financial burdens. Even the idea of a sentimental involvement was far from my mind. The war was still on and I had one last mission to fulfil.

Berlin was my target.

'You will be dropped there to await the Allies!' Dereck had told me a few days earlier. 'We need someone on the spot. I'll expect you in London.'

Reluctantly I obeyed, convinced that this last drop would be the end of me. Two or three weeks after meeting Geneviève, I returned to London, but my morale was low; as in Paris, the atmosphere had not been inspiring.

It was not easy to walk through an American zone of Paris in English uniform. The Americans had piled up grudges of all kinds during the time they had been stationed in England, and on every occasion they ventilated them in my presence. Incidents were purposely provoked, and when US servicemen bullied me their officers looked on, smiling, without interfering.

I spent long hours in Drancy, a camp where real or alleged collaborators were imprisoned. I had decided to help to make good the glaring injustices commited in purge operations, and I was able to obtain the release of several persons imprisoned for reasons of revenge.

The necessity for merciless purges was loudly advocated by certain party spokesmen, by individuals who had been out of the country and therefore ignorant of the conditions prevailing under the Occupation, and by last-minute converts anxious to cover up their former activities. In this context, human behaviour was seen at its worst.

I went to London, leaving Geneviève to her career as an actress, and plunged body and soul into the preparation of my mission.

Dereck had been promoted and had left London. I visited my children, frustrated at not being able to foresee their future: further, because of the top secrecy of my job I saw nobody and led a hermit's existence.

'Why not write a film script?' suggested an officer with whom I was working. 'Go and see Christine, she is secretary to a producer I know. If she's interested, you can shake off your black mood with a mushy love-story.'

It was an idea. That same evening I made my way to her address. It was hard going. London was blanketed in a thick fog. While I was groping blindly to find the bell, she came out to have a look at the weather and invited me in.

I explained the reason for my visit. She was enthusiastic, and we decided that she would type my script from dictation. Knowing the professional way to present it, she would be able to give it the right twist.

'You must concoct' she insisted, 'a love-story under the Occupation, the patriotic and pure French girl dominated by a Teutonic lover, or something like that.'

I shrugged my shoulders, and agreed. A love-story requires a heroine. In describing her, I adorned her with all the virtues.

Then I realised that I had unconsciously taken Géneviève as my model.

Fate, for the second time, played her part. I cabled Geneviève:

'Marry me'. She answered with one word: 'Yes!' So I took leave and returned to Paris to spend a few days with her.

The Von Runstedt offensive had made progress. The Berlin mission was first postponed and then cancelled. I was overjoyed to remain in France.

The days passed filled with measures to be taken to dissolve the Line: applications for decorations, official visits, and thanks all round.

After a stay in Tarbes, gall-bladder trouble confined me to bed.

Geneviève was nursing me. One afternoon, unannounced, a high-ranking British officer came to see me. He had arrived from London to discuss important matters. First and foremost, he told me that I had been awarded the Order of the British Empire for military services.

'You deserve it', he added, cutting short my thanks. 'That's why I came to suggest you should carry on. You were supposed to await our troops in Berlin. Well, they'll arrive there shortly. So why not settle there officially? The capital of the Reich will be an observation post of importance. With your German and experience you'll be a valuable chap.'

'Thanks and all that', I replied, 'but once the war is over, it's good-bye to the army. I want to get back to civilian life and forget about war. Let me tell you what friends had prepared for me in Tarbes: the hanging of eight militiamen on the bandstand. They thought I'd enjoy it. No thanks. Believe me, I am through!'

My visitor smiled. 'The job would probably get you a knighthood', he said.

'Oh, for God's sake! The answer is still no. Once this bloody war is over I've finished.'

'You forget', he said, raising his voice, 'that you enlisted for the duration. Even if the war ends in Europe there's still Asia.

I'll see to it that you get a one-way ticket to Japan.'

A bitter note was creeping into our conversation. At that moment, Geneviève walked into the room with two cups of tea made the English way. The interruption was heaven-sent. The three of us relaxed and chatted as if nothing had happened.

Taking his leave, the officer turned to Geneviève and exclaimed in French: *'Cherchez la femme!* Tell him to apply for demobilisation! Providing he gives me his word never to disclose anything to harm the Service, I'll recommend his release.'

He kept his word and so did I. I received my demob papers, plus a warm letter of thanks for services rendered.

Contact with the Service ceased abruptly. Although I met Dereck twice after, general topics only were discussed. What a pity! He is an outstanding person and I think he might have become a Buddhist monk under different circumstances.

17

Mystique! That is what my two daughters called this most uncommon man. The name fitted like a glove.

The children had joined me in Paris. Heidi, their mother, had remarried in England, and I had married Geneviève. She introduced me to Mystique.

He never tried to hide himself in mystery. Quite the contrary. He was hearty and gay, with a ready smile. A genial, bright-eyed man, with a strong, youthful figure, and a face with regular features framed by a well-trimmed beard. I met Mystique one Sunday afternoon at his house in Passy, a residential district of Paris.

I quickly became what may be called a disciple. I plied him with questions, told him of my worries and my attempts to find a solution to the many problems of a world in turmoil.

I had a lot of trouble in disentangling my highly involved financial situation to meet the needs of my family, and also to fathom the reason of my existence upon earth. What was fate, what were my abilities, what about the vanity-fair all around me? I was groping in the dark, in the grip of the necessity of earning a living and the frustrated desire to escape from realities.

Settling down to a daily routine was not easy. More than once I yearned for adventure, wild rides and great open spaces reminiscent of the recent past.

My daughters too had difficulty in adjusting to a family life totally different from the one they had experienced in England. Fortunately, they got on well with Geneviève and, after a baby brother was born, problems subsided.

In order to start the plant anew, I had to fight hard, particularly against all kinds of financial racketeers. However, my unflagging efforts were not in vain and I was able to bring to the daily routine a certain hard-won wisdom.

It was Mystique who explained one day the difference between well-being and well-existing.

'To exist well implies a fulfilment of desires, and man is so made that desire breeds desire, and fulfilment seems therefore out of reach. Well-being means an awareness of the Essential. One behaves intelligently. One designs one's destiny thanks to creative action, generating joy. Creative action is the expression of Harmony on the chosen plane.'

Mystique and his wife, totally devoted to him, soon agreed to leave Paris and settle in a cottage near my mountain home at Amphion. Whenever we stayed there, we spent long hours together discussing the different aspects of truth.

Meetings were organised, and many who joined us contributed to an understanding of Life and the laws of existence.

A couple visited us frequently and a close relationship developed during the following months, a relationship which can be compared to a magic spell.

The woman I shall call Euryale and the man Fidèle. The word occult, as I understand it, means 'not immediately

139

perceptible' and the word magic relates to forces not yet acknowledged scientifically.

Euryale was beautiful, intelligent and cultured. She dazzled most men. She dazzled me.

Of Slavonic origin, she had studied the secrets of the Shamans, the Siberian priests and medicine-men, who hold widespread powers through their occult links with animistic entities residing in the bowels of the earth. She seemed to have an excellent relationship with this world of elemental forces, and knew how to charm both men and women whenever she wanted.

Well versed in Hinduism, a remarkable poet, and practising ascetic excercises, she was certainly the strangest woman I have ever met, and her husband was completely under her spell.

'She is a goddess! Only the blind and ignorant don't realise it' he assured me.

Fidèle was quite a personality too. A gallant soldier, he finished the war as a general, after performing one of the most heroic feats of the period. During the Occupation, he had succeeded in sending to England — using the Line as a channel — some highly valuable documents which enabled the RAF to destroy a vital German rocket centre.

When appointed to an important military position, he faithfully followed all advice Euryale gave him.

'You'll reach the top of the pyramid' she promised. 'But you must be worthy of it, and only he who overcomes all limitations is worthy.'

In her view, overcoming all limitations had to be complete.

'Ties emotionally binding anybody to anything had to be severed' she explained. 'The forces of Nature only obey those free of sentimentality and all desire.'

'I am', swore Fidèle.

He had left his first wife, but to comply with Euryale's teaching, he severed all ties with his children, refused to meet former friends and comrades-at-arms, and only associated with those approved by Euryale. And Euryale approved only of those who admired her brilliant mind.

140

I should point out that Euryale, guided by genuine knowledge, misused her very real powers — all the more regrettable since she must have been aware of what she was doing.

She knew I was on the lookout for something fundamental, and suggested I should follow Fidèle's example, pretending that if I trusted her she would provide the solution to all my difficulties.

By subtle hints, she attempted to tarnish Geneviève's image and she mocked my admiration for Mystique though always in an amiable way. Mystique, aware of the fact, never reacted.

'Euryale had been initiated into many secrets of our world', he said, 'but her magic powers veer from white to black. So she may take advantage of her power to reach questionable objectives. It is up to you to discover what has to be rejected. It is not for me to prevent you from learning what is right or wrong. Your choice must be free from any outside influence. The decision is yours.'

'But,' I protested, 'Euryale has warned me clairvoyantly that my intended trip to Buenos Aires to visit my aging parents would have evil consequences affecting both my family and myself.'

'It is up to you Frédéric', repeated Mystique. 'You must be aware, and since you met Garcia you are aware that there are more things than our philosophy admits. Find out what is at stake. If you follow, you will merely obey. Obedience however is not understanding, and my role consists in helping you towards understanding.'

I hesitated. Fidèle, during a walk in the park bordering a lake whose waters sparkled in the summer sunshine, noticed my hesitation.

'Frédéric' he said, 'in another existence we were brothers. I know this can't be proved, but it is true. Euryale confirmed it. For God's sake follow the advice of the one I call a Goddess!'

'And supposing she is not a Goddess?'

'You fool! The guru holds out his hand and you reject it. Be sensible!' I left for Buenos Aires. No disaster befell me or my family. The fact that I had decided in complete independence had freed me.

Our meetings with the couple became less frequent. When they did occur, I realised that Fidèle was being turned into a robot, serving the Goddess.

My friendship for Fidèle was profound. He had been straight and sincere. Yet to prove to himself that he was able to overcome any limitation, he violated his own nature and adopted an attitude opposed to his former one. He had reached a stage of pitiful decline and accepted it with a cheerless smile.

How did it happen? The answer is not simple. Travellers to far-off lands know that it is possible to walk on glowing embers without getting burnt, providing one accepts the Sorcerer's power. This acceptance releases occult forces.

Euryale had such powers. She told me once that only a little know-how is needed to direct these vital forces.

Yes, Euryale had them; and maybe she lost them. Fidèle, at last aware that he had destroyed his life, let himself die. Euryale is still alive and is paying the price of misused knowledge. Yet one should not judge her too harshly. I knew her well. I saw her in action. Fascinated by her gifts, I am inclined not to defend what cannot be defended, but to draw a lesson therefrom. I acknowledge I owe her a lot. Any teaching carries a fertile seed if based on true cognition, even when misused.

Only those are free who act according to genuine feelings and the deep, true instincts. Euryale taught me to see people not as they physically appear but as they truly are, beyond the visible. This permits an attunement — I have experienced it — which harmonises all human relationships.

One can only come to know such attunement by casting away the crutches formed by habit of false concepts. Life, by its constraints, teaches us how to get rid of them, and therefore should be considered a laboratory, and not purgatory.

18

In the years immediately following the war, I reached a totally different outlook on life even though I did not realise it at the time.

I knew that only a miraculous combination of circumstances had enabled me to avoid certain death, and had led me to discover the true values of life. Now I had responsibilities of my own which must be used to help others discover them. How to accomplish this task, how to pass on this knowledge that destiny had taught me? This was the question.

It took me some time to find out. It is not enough to communicate one's experience verbally, nor to write a novel or a play about it.

Spiritual consciousness can only be achieved if the experience takes its meaning in a new consciousness born through joys, sorrows and dangers. It can only be achieved if one is ready to discard all prior beliefs, even in a well-meaning Providence, or alert guardian angel.

The initial discarding of beliefs which have afforded a feeling of security arouses agonising doubts which no knowledge can dispel; later, if one accepts the test, one is led to a larger vision of the world.

I have tried, and am still trying, to teach others to share this view from above, in order to rise above one's problems and relate them to an overall situation and there to find a solution as yet unthought of. That is why I began — under Mystique's guidance — the study of the Great Tradition which had impregnated the spiritual adventure of the Occident.

The Great Tradition transmits the quintessence of all human experience. It weaves a luminous thread linking the source to the issue, as all that exists — be it dense or subtle, formulated or unformulated — plunges its roots into what has been, in order to become what it shall be. Carried forward by occult initiatory currents, the Great Tradition has had considerable impact on Western thought and culture.

I had access to Mystique's library and its rare contents. We met many people from all corners of the world. I discovered Zen Buddhism, Theosophy, Hinduism. I studied Hermetism, and particularly Alchemy. I discovered the Philosophy of Numbers which Pythagoras brought back from Egypt. I entered into the teachings of Ancient Greece as divulged in the small and great Mysteries of Hellas. And thus I passed from one state of awareness to another enabling me to discover the hidden reasons behind human strife, and those behind the last world conflict.

Before leaving the Service, during the period of preparation for my mission to Berlin, I had access to documents that opened new, hitherto unsuspected horizons. I was able to study the metaphysical aspects of a philosophy based on power, which — of Asiatic origin — inspired the Teutonic Knights and then the military caste of Imperial Germany, as well as the National Socialist prophets.

It is by no means certain that the coming generation of Germans has freed itself from the spell exerted by power in whatever form it may take, military, political, or economic. It is a magnetic pole of attraction for men strong or weak, here and elsewhere.

Euryale, as I have said, unveiled the entrance to a mystic world. She insisted that the explanation of a new dimension of our universe could only be undertaken if we forget our personal ambitions. Today, I understand the reason why in a distant past, initiation was reserved only for those chosen ones who had given evidence of their cognition and proved their good faith. It is too easy to misuse powers generated by teachings which reveal secrets that can awaken the hidden energies of Nature; this applies to communities and individuals.

I had witnessed the impact of these forces towards good or evil, according to the channel they were able to use and how they were directed.

I now make it a rule to observe the world impartially, to watch the impulsive actions of those swayed by slogans and theories.

Much is to be discovered in this world, where questions and answers intermingle and men switch from obverse to reverse without knowing which side is right.

'Hazard makes men's happiness', Racine said. I believe man enjoys those adventures where the unexpected upsets the expected, giving him no time to understand what is going on. He can thus elude the logical conclusion that to know enables him to foresee. Knowledge may help him to right the helm of a drifting boat, but it is wiser to learn the laws ruling the currents and winds during the trip.

Man wants to be free but then discovers he is a robot. Professor Monod states: 'Man is a machine made of molecules'. And there are man-made machines which calculate faster than he does, which compose music, or even poetry.

Are we really just that? The robot in me protests, 'I wish to be a human being.' Why? Because robots want to conquer so as to dominate. The true human being meditates to discover the reasons for his existence so as to be able to fulfil his destiny.

What is his destiny? To lift the veil woven by centuries of robots, hiding the essential, offering many immediately congenial solutions.

I have heard about a Paradise Lost. Lost where? In the heavens or upon earth? Another illusion woven by the robots! We are on earth to govern our kingdom. The robots within us should be our loyal servants, helping us to achieve our destiny. Instead, we are burdened with the weight of their inhumanity, which acts and plans in ways divorced from the imperatives of everlasting wisdom. Man is no robot!

To lower human dignity in order to dominate was Euryale's intention. She sought to dominate in order to assert her power. Others did and do the same although they may choose different means.

The reverse, to act in a perfect symbiosis with the laws of Nature, to serve it so as to promote Harmony bringing joy, generated by creative action, irons out all conflicts in perfect accord with Life. That is what gives a meaning to existence, reflecting the cosmic plan.

Before writing the word 'End' to this last chapter, I would like to give a brief summary of what happened to some of my friends mentioned in the course of this story.

Fernand, for reasons unknown, committed suicide long after the war. The British officer I found in the gutter in Marseille reached the rank of general. I met him immediately after the Liberation of Paris. He told me that he moved heaven and earth to find out who I was but without success.

Emilio, the Italian friend of Fernand, was appointed Minister in his country. The Polish airman was shot down over Germany. Certain parcels we had helped to reach freedom came to see me or wrote to say thank you. Others ignored us and others again did not bother to give any sign of life.

Garcia disappeared. He told me that he was going to Lebanon to join a Master living among the Druse in their mountains. For all I know, he may still be there.

Tristan and his family are doing well, but live too much with their recollections of a heroic period. Jacques is married and has several children. As for the countless companions whose names I did not mention, many have died, others live on peacefully, while others cling to memories of an extraordinary adventure that gave meaning to their lives.

Mystique died in my arms, and before leaving his body he handed me a rose that Geneviève had placed in a vase at his bedside.

'Meditate on this symbol,' he said. 'It is more than an image of beauty. Manifest under all skies the Good and the Beautiful, reflect the love of the Eternal; you will fulfil your destiny and find your way to Happiness. Such is the secret of Life.'

EPILOGUE

The meaning of the story I have told is revealed in the words of Shakespeare:

'To master Nature, obey her.'

His words require no comment, but are the opposite of the convenient statement one should leave to the Sense of History — with a capital H — the full responsibility of man's destiny. The sense of History is a false idea. History is marked by confusion; even historians of good faith can only relate events they have not personally observed.

Men make History, and not History men. This is the message contained in this story. I have told it as honestly as I could.